THE BATSFORD BOOK
OF ROMANTIC POETRY

THE BATSFORD BOOK OF ROMANTIC POETRY

Edited by Samuel Carr

B. T. BATSFORD LTD. LONDON

ISBN 0 7134 3903 3

Photoset in 12 on 13pt Linotype Bembo by
Tek-Art Ltd, London, SE20
and printed in Great Britain by
The Pitman Press Ltd,
Bath, Somerset
for the publishers
B. T. Batsford Ltd,
4 Fitzhardinge Street
London W1H 0AH

Contents

The Illustrations 7
Introduction 9

JOHN DYER *The Yellow Barn* 11
THOMAS GRAY *April* 12
THOMAS GRAY *Twilight* 13
WILLIAM MASON *English Plants* 14
WILLIAM GILPIN *Sea-Fowl* 15
ERASMUS DARWIN *Fuseli's Nightmare* 16
JOHN CUNNINGHAM *Pale Regent of the Sky* 17
WILLIAM COWPER *Yardley Oak* 19
WILLIAM COWPER *The Wood in Winter* 21
THOMAS CHATTERTON *Fragment* 22
GEORGE CRABBE *Neap Tide* 23
GEORGE CRABBE *Summer Sea* 24
GEORGE CRABBE *Seashore* 25
WILLIAM BLAKE *To the Evening Star* 28
WILLIAM BLAKE *Auguries of Innocence* 28
WILLIAM BLAKE *Song of Spring* 30
ROBERT BURNS *The Primrose* 32
ROBERT BURNS *Ye Flowery Banks* 33
ROBERT BURNS *Now Spring Has Clad The Grove in Green* 34
WILLIAM BOWLES *Bamborough Castle* 36
WILLIAM BOWLES *Fonthill Abbey* 38
WILLIAM WORDSWORTH *Lines composed a few miles above Tintern Abbey* 39
WILLIAM WORDSWORTH *Gordale* 46
WILLIAM WORDSWORTH *Inside of King's College Chapel, Cambridge* 46
WILLIAM WORDSWORTH *Staffa, the Island* 47
SIR WALTER SCOTT *My Romantic Theme* 48
SIR WALTER SCOTT *November* 49
ROBERT SOUTHEY *Written on the First of December* 50
W. S. LANDOR *Autumnal Song* 52
JOHN WILSON *Written on the Banks of Wastwater During a Calm* 52
CHARLES LAMB *Written at Cambridge* 53
THOMAS MOORE *'Oft, in the Stilly Night'* 54
LEIGH HUNT *The Grasshopper and the Cricket* 55
THOMAS CAMPBELL *The Last Man* 56
WILLIAM BLAKE *From: America, a Prophecy* 60

SAMUEL TAYLOR COLERIDGE From: Hymn before Sun-rise, in the Vale of Chamouni   63

LEIGH HUNT A House and Grounds   65

HENRY KIRKE WHITE Description of a Summer's Eve   66

THOMAS LOVE PEACOCK The Sun-dial   68

MARY RUSSELL MITFORD Written in July 1824   69

SAMUEL TAYLOR COLERIDGE Kubla Khan   70

LORD BYRON Norman Abbey   72

LORD BYRON Stormy Coast   77

THOMAS STOKES SALMON Stonehenge   78

FRIEDRICH VON SCHILLER Song of the Alps   81

LORD BYRON The Château of Chillon   82

PERCY BYSSHE SHELLEY The Cloud   83

PERCY BYSSHE SHELLEY To the Nile   84

PERCY BYSSHE SHELLEY To the Moon   84

GEORGE DARLEY 'While the Moon Decks Herself'   85

PERCY BYSSHE SHELLEY Ozymandias   87

JOHN KEBLE Autumn Leaves   88

JOHN CLARE To the Clouds   89

JOHN CLARE Sudden Shower   90

JOHN CLARE Description of a Thunder-storm   91

FELICIA DOROTHEA HEMANS Foliage   94

WILLIAM CULLEN BRYANT March   95

JOHN KEATS To Ailsa Rock   96

JOHN KEATS Ode to a Nightingale   97

JOHN KEATS To Autumn   100

JOHN KEATS On the Sea   101

HARTLEY COLERIDGE There was a cot…   102

THOMAS HOOD Lear   103

WILLIAM BARNES Clouds   106

THOMAS LOVELL BEDDOES Lines   107

THOMAS LOVELL BEDDOES The New-born Star   108

SAMUEL PALMER Shoreham   110

CHARLES TENNYSON TURNER A Summer Twilight   111

EDGAR ALLAN POE The City in the Sea   112

HENRY DAVID THOREAU To the Mountains   116

CHRISTINA ROSSETTI My Dream   118

EMILY BRONTË Mild the Mist upon the Hill   122

Index of Poets   123

Index of Artists   124

The Illustrations

COLOUR

page

61 'Thus wept the Angel voice...' From *America* (1793) by William Blake (1757-1816). *The Fitzwilliam Museum, Cambridge*

62 The Source of the Arveiron. From the watercolour by Francis Towne (1740-1816). *The Victoria and Albert Museum, London*

79 Stonehenge (detail). From the painting by John Constable (1776-1837). *The Victoria and Albert Museum, London*

80 The Devil's Bridge, St Gothard. From the painting by J.M.W. Turner (1775-1851). Private Collection. (*Transparency: Thomas Agnew and Sons Ltd., London*)

BLACK AND WHITE

frontispiece: Landscape with Rainbow (detail). From the painting by Joseph Wright (1734-1797). *Derby: Musuem and Art Gallery*

page

15 Beaumont's Green Oak. From the drawing by James Ward (1769-1825). *Castle Museum, Norwich*

16 The Nightmare. From the painting by Henry Fuseli (1741-1825). *The Detroit Institute of Arts*

18 The Old Oak. From the painting by by John Crome (1768-1821). *The National Gallery of Canada, Ottawa*

24 The Sea near Brighton. From the painting by John Constable (1776-1837). *The Tate Gallery, London*

27 Coast Scene. From the watercolour by George Barret Jnr. (1767-1842). *Reproduced by gracious permission of HM The Queen*

37 Bamburgh Castle. From the painting by Thomas Girtin (1775-1802). *The Tate Gallery, London*

38 Fonthill Abbey, Wiltshire. Engraved by J. Barnett after a drawing by J. C. Buckler (1770-1851). *From the Gentleman's Magazine* (1822)

42 Tintern Abbey. From the painting by John Crome (1768-1821). *The Castle Museum, Norwich*

53 Cambridge. From a print (1793) by W. and J. Walker after a drawing by J. Walker, figures by Edward Burney (1760-1848)

56- The Last Man. From the painting by John Martin (1789-1854).
57 *Merseyside County Art Galleries*

64 The Grove. From the painting by John Constable (1789-1837). *The Tate Gallery, London*

67 Evening. From the watercolour by Samuel Palmer (1805-1881). *The Castle Museum, Norwich*

73 Landscape with Ruins by Night. From the painting by Joseph Wright (1734-1797). *The Graves Art Gallery, Sheffield*

7

77   'Storm, View on the Coast of Hastings'. From an illustration by David Cox (1783-1859) to his *Treatise on Landscape Painting* (1813-14). *The British Library*

82   The Castle of Chillon. From the watercolour by John Varley (1778-1842). *The Victoria and Albert Museum, London*

85   'The Face of the Moon'. From the picture by John Russell (1745-1806). *The City of Birmingham Museum and Art Gallery*

86   'The Artist moved by the Grandeur of Antique Fragments'. From the drawing by Henry Fuseli (1748-1825). *Kunsthaus, Zürich*

89   Cloud Study. From the sketch by John Constable (1776-1837). *The Victoria and Albert Museum, London*

90   'Rain, Heath Scene'. From an illustration by David Cox (1783-1859) to his *Treatise on Landscape Painting* (1813-14). *The British Library*

94   'Nightingale Valley, Leigh Woods, Bristol'. From the painting by Francis Danby (1793-1861). *Bristol Art Gallery*

104-105   'Mont Blanc and the Arve near Sallenches'. From the watercolour by John Robert Cozens (1752-1797). *The British Museum*

114-115   'The Enchanted Castle'. From the painting by Francis Danby (1793-1861). *The Victoria and Albert Museum, London*

117   'In Nature's Wonderland' (detail). From the painting by Thomas Doughty (1793-1856). *The Detroit Institute of Arts (Founders' Society Purchase: The Gibbs-Williams Fund)*

120-121   Bushey Churchyard. From the watercolour by William Henry Hunt (1790-1864). *The Victoria and Albert Museum, London*

124   'Natural Scenery'. An illustration by Humphry Repton (1752-1818) to his *Observations on Landscape Gardening* (1803). *The British Library*

The front endpaper is reproduced from the watercolour, 'The Harvest Field', by J. S. Cotman (1782-1842) (*Leeds City Art Gallery*). The back endpaper is reproduced from the painting, 'Shipwreck', by P. J. de Loutherbourg (1740-1812) (*Kunsthistorisches Museum, Vienna*).

INTRODUCTION

If there is one sentiment on which writers about the Romantic movement agree it is the elusiveness of any satisfactory definition of their subject. The best anyone can do is to fall back on a phrase like Baudelaire's *'une manière de sentir'*, which means much what one wants it to mean. Whether that way of feeling resulted in a preoccupation with the particular, as John Piper believed, with 'the inner life, the raptures and fears and aspirations and fantasies of the soul in solitude' as Lord David Cecil held, or in the 'importance which they attached to the imagination', in Maurice Bowra's phrase, is less important than it appears since the contemporary views of the Romantics themselves were as conflicting as their critics' were later to be.

Can it at the same time be true that 'This world of Imagination is the world of Eternity' and that 'To Particularize is the Alone Distinction of Merit'? Blake believed it was. Or that 'All good poetry is the spontaneous overflow of powerful feelings', as Wordsworth claimed in his Preface to *Lyrical Ballads and* that (as Coleridge commented in *Biographia Literaria*) Wordsworth's own poetry reflects, more objectively, 'The perfect truth of nature in his images and descriptions, as taken immediately from nature…'? Such apparent contradictions could be multiplied.

The practice of the artists no less than that of the poets reflects the same uncertainty as to whether it is the subject itself, their own reaction to it, or a free-wheeling essay of the imagination far removed from the physical world, which should be their proper concern. Constable's view was: 'The world is wide; no two days are alike nor even two hours, neither were there ever two leaves of a tree alike since the beginning of the world; and the genuine productions of art, like those of nature, are all distinct from one another'. What has such concern with objective exactitude in common with the airy or apocalyptic visions of a Turner, a Samuel Palmer or a John Martin?

Nor does the language used by the poets, or the date at which they wrote, provide much help towards arriving at a definition of Romanticism. The year 1798, when *Lyrical Ballads* appeared, used sometimes to be cited as marking the beginning of the movement, yet the manner of Thomson and Gray, of Cowper and Crabbe disguises a way of looking at nature which often had more in common with that of Shelley and Wordsworth, Keats and Coleridge than with that of their poetic predecessors. This was evidently a feeling shared by Turner, who, when he sought an epigraph for one of his paintings, was more likely to find it in Milton or Pope than in the writers of his own day, whose outlook might be thought to be more in tune with his own.

This particular anthology has the dual aim of collecting together poems and pictures which are admirable for their own sake and of showing how writers and artists have reacted to the same subject. What is there in common between Byron and Constable's feelings about the Ocean, between Wordsworth and Crome's reaction to Tintern Abbey, between a bird's nest seen by W.H. Hunt and by John Clare? It might be hard to say, apart from that indefinable '*manière de sentir*' noted by Baudelaire.

The editor of a collection like this one is generally criticised for being too conventional; if not that, then for being too concerned with the unfamiliar for its own sake. The present editor cannot hope to escape such criticism. How should he when the choice is necessarily a personal one, and the reader will have his own favourites and antipathies? The most he can hope is that his choice may give more pleasure than vexation, and that the juxtaposition of poems and pictures on related subjects may suggest a further way of regarding Romanticism.

The Yellow Barn

From: Elegy

The morning's fair, the lusty Sun
With ruddy cheeks begins to run;
And early birds, that wing the skies,
Sweetly sing to see him rise.
  I am resolved, this charming day,
In the open field to stray;
And have no roof above my head,
But that whereon the gods do tread.
Before the yellow barn I see
A beautiful variety
Of strutting cocks, advancing stout,
And flirting empty chaff about,
Hens, ducks and geese, and all their brood,
And turkeys gobbling for their food;
While rustics thresh the wealthy floor,
And tempt them all to crowd the door.
  What a fair pace does Nature show!
Augusta, wipe thy dusty brow;
A landscape wide salutes my sight,
Of shady vales, and mountains bright;
And azure heavens I behold,
And clouds of silver and of gold.
And now into the fields I go,
Where thousand flaming flowers grow;
And every neighbouring hedge I greet,
With honeysuckles smelling sweet.

JOHN DYER (1699-1758)

April
From: Ode to the Pleasure arising from Vicissitude

Now the golden Morn aloft
  Waves her dew-bespangled wing;
With vermeil cheek and whisper soft
  She woo's the tardy spring:
Till April starts, and calls around
The sleeping fragrance from the ground,
And lightly o'er the living scene
Scatters his freshest, tenderest green.

New-born flocks in rustic dance
  Frisking ply their feeble feet.
Forgetful of their wintry trance
  The birds his presence greet.
But chief the Sky-lark warbles high
His trembling thrilling ecstasy;
And, less'ning from the dazzled sight,
Melts into air and liquid light.

Yesterday the sullen year
  Saw the snowy whirlwind fly;
Mute was the musick of the air,
  The Herd stood drooping by:
Their raptures now that wildly flow,
No yesterday, nor morrow know;
'Tis Man alone that Joy descries
With forward and reverted eyes.

THOMAS GRAY (1716-1771)

Twilight

From: Elegy in a Country Churchyard

The Curfew tolls the knell of parting day,
The lowing herd wind slowly o'er the lea,
The plowman homeward plods his weary way,
And leaves the world to darkness and to me.

Now fades the glimmering landscape on the sight,
And all the air a solemn stillness holds,
Save where the beetle wheels his droning flight,
And drowsy tinklings lull the distant folds;

Save that from yonder ivy-mantled tow'r
The mopeing owl does to the moon complain
Of such, as wand'ring near her secret bow'r,
Molest her ancient solitary reign.

Beneath those rugged elms, that yew-tree's shade,
Where heaves the turf in many a mould'ring heap,
Each in his narrow cell for ever laid,
The rude Forefathers of the hamlet sleep.

The breezy call of incense-breathing Morn,
The swallow twitt'ring from the straw-built shed,
The cock's shrill clarion, or the ecchoing horn,
No more shall rouse them from their lowly bed.

THOMAS GRAY (1716-1771)

English Plants

From: English Garden

   Nor are the plants which England calls her own
Few or unlovely, that, with laurel join'd
And kindred foliage of perennial green,
Will form a close-knit curtain. Shrubs there are
Of bolder growth, that, at the call of Spring,
Burst forth in blossom'd fragrance: lilacs rob'd
In snow-white innocence, or purple pride;
The sweet syringa yielding but in scent
To the rich orange; or the woodbine wild
That loves to hang, on barren boughs remote,
Her wreaths of flowery perfume. These beside,
Myriads, that here the Muse neglects to name,
Will add a vernal lustre to thy veil.

   And what if chance collects the varied tribes,
Yet fear not thou but unexpected charms
Will from their union start. But if our song
Supply one precept here, it bids retire
Each leaf of deeper dye, and lift in front
Foliage of paler verdure, so to spread
A canvass, which when touch'd by Autumn's hand
Shall gleam with dusky gold, or russet rays.
But why prepare for her funereal hand
That canvass? she but comes to dress thy shades,
As lovelier victims for their wintry tomb.
Rather to flowery Spring, to Summer bright,
Thy labour consecrate; their laughing reign,
The youth, the manhood of the growing year,
Deserves that labour, and rewards its pain.
Yet, heedful ever of that ruthless time
When Winter shakes their stems, preserve a file
With everduring leaf to brave his arm,
And deepening spread their undiminish'd gloom.

WILLIAM MASON (1724-1797)

14

Sea-Fowl
From: Landscape Painting

Far up yon river, opening to the sea,
Just where the distant coast extends a curve,
A lengthened train of sea-fowl urge their flight.
Observe their files! In what exact array
The dark battalion floats, distinctly seen
Before yon silver cliff! Now, now, they reach
That lonely beacon; now are lost again
In yon dark cloud. How pleasing is the sight!
The forest-glade from its wild, timorous herd,
Receives not richer ornament, than here
From birds this lonely sea-view.

REV. WILLIAM GILPIN (1724-1804)

Beaumont's Green Oak. *James Ward*

The Nightmare. *Henry Fuseli*

Fuseli's Nightmare

So on his NIGHTMARE through the evening fog
Flits the squab Fiend o'er fen, and lake, and bog;
Seeks some love-wilder'd Maid with sleep oppress'd,
Alights, and grinning sits upon her breast.
—Such as of late amid the murky sky
Was marked by FUSELI'S poetic eye;
Whose daring tints, with SHAKESPEAR'S happiest grace,
Gave to the airy phantom form and place.—
Back o'er her pillow sinks her blushing head,
Her snow-white limbs hang helpless from the bed;
While with quick sighs, and suffocative breath,
Her interrupted heart-pulse swims in death.
—Then shrieks of captur'd towns, and widow's tears,
Pale lovers stretch'd upon their blood-stain'd biers,
The headlong precipice that thwarts her flight,
The trackless desert, the cold starless night,
And stern-eyed Murderer with his knife behind,
In dread succession agonize her mind.

O'er her fair limbs convulsive tremors fleet,
Start in her hands, and struggle in her feet;
In vain to scream with quivering lips she tries,
And strains in palsy'd lips her tremulous eyes;
In vain she *wills* to run, fly, swim, walk, creep;
The WILL presides not in the bower of SLEEP.
—On her fair bosom sits the Demon-Ape,
Erect, and balances his bloated shape;
Rolls in their marble orbs his Gorgon-eyes
And drinks with leathern ears her tender cries.

ERASMUS DARWIN (1731–1802)

Pale Regent of the Sky
From: Contemplation: A Night Piece

The sweets, that bending o'er their banks,
    From sultry Day declin'd,
Revive in little velvet ranks,
    And scent the western wind.

The Moon, preceded by the breeze
    That bade the clouds retire,
Appears amongst the tufted trees
    A Phoenix nest on fire.

But soft—the golden glow subsides!
    Her chariot mounts on high!
And now, in silent pomp, she rides
    Pale regent of the sky!

JOHN CUNNINGHAM (1729-1773)

The Old Oak. *John Crome*

Yardley Oak

Survivor sole, and hardly such, of all
That once liv'd here thy brethren, at my birth
(Since which I number three-score winters past)
A shatter'd veteran, hollow-trunk'd perhaps
As now, and with excoriate forks deform,
Relicts of ages! Could a mind, imbued
With truth from heav'n, created thing adore,
I might with rev'rence kneel and worship thee.
   It seems idolatry with some excuse
When our fore-father Druids in their oaks
Imagin'd sanctity. The conscience yet
Unpurified by an authentic act
Of amnesty, the meed of blood divine,
Lov'd not the light, but gloomy into gloom
Of thickest shades, like Adam after taste
Of fruit proscrib'd, as to a refuge, fled.
   Thou wast a bauble once; a cup and ball,
Which babes might play with; and the thievish jay
Seeking her food, with ease might have purloin'd
The auburn nut that held thee, swallowing down
Thy yet close-folded latitude of boughs
And all thine embryo vastness, at a gulp.
But Fate thy growth decreed: autumnal rains
Beneath thy parent tree mellow'd the soil
Design'd thy cradle, and a skipping deer
With pointed hoof dibbling the glebe, prepar'd
The soft receptacle in which secure
Thy rudiments should sleep the winter through.

   * * *

And Time hath made thee what thou art—a cave
For owls to roost in. Once thy spreading boughs
O'erhung the champain; and the numerous flock
That graz'd it stood beneath that ample cope
Uncrowded, yet safe-shelter'd from the storm.
No flock frequents thee now. Thou hast outliv'd
Thy popularity and art become
(Unless verse rescues thee awhile) a thing
Forgotten, as the foliage of thy youth.
    While thus through all the stages thou hast push'd
Of treeship, first a seedling hid in grass,
Then twig, then sapling, and, as century roll'd
Slow after century, a giant bulk
Of girth enormous, with moss-cushion'd root
Upheav'd above the soil, and sides imboss'd
With prominent wens globose, till at the last
The rottenness, which time is charg'd t'inflict
On other mighty ones, found also thee—
★   ★   ★
    Thine arms have left thee. Winds have rent them off
Long since, and rovers of the forest wild
With bow and shaft have burnt them. Some have left
A splinter'd stump bleach'd to a snowy white;
And some memorial none where once they grew.
Yet life still lingers in thee, and puts forth
Proof not contemptible of what she can,
Even where death predominates. The spring
Thee finds not less alive to her sweet force
Than yonder upstarts of the neighbour wood,
So much thy juniors, who their birth receiv'd
Half a millennium since the date of thine.

WILLIAM COWPER (1731-1800)

20

The Wood in Winter

From: The Task

The night was winter in his roughest mood;
The morning sharp and clear. But now at noon
Upon the southern side of the slant hills,
And where the woods fence off the northern blast,
The season smiles, resigning all its rage,
And has the warmth of May. The vault is blue
Without a cloud, and white without a speck
The dazzling splendour of the scene below.
Again the harmony comes o'er the vale;
And through the trees I view th'embattled tow'r
Whence all the music. I again perceive
The soothing influence of the wafted strains,
And settle in soft musings as I tread
The walk, still verdant, under oaks and elms,
Whose outspread branches overarch the glade.
The roof, though moveable through all its length
As the wind sways it, has yet well suffic'd,
And, intercepting in their silent fall
The frequent flakes, has kept a path for me.
No noise is here, or none that hinders thought.
The redbreast warbles still, but is content
With slender notes, and more than half suppress'd:
Pleas'd with his solitude, and flitting light
From spray to spray, where'er he rests he shakes
From many a twig the pendent drops of ice,
That tinkle in the wither'd leaves below.
Stillness, accompanied with sounds so soft,
Charms more than silence. Meditation here
May think down hours to moments. Here the heart
May give an useful lesson to the head,
And learning wiser grow without his books.

WILLIAM COWPER (1731–1800)

Fragment

Attributed to Ecca, Bishop of Hereford A.D. *557*
Translated by Rowley

When azure skies is veiled in robes of night,
   When glimmering dewdrops 'stound the traveller's
     eyne,
When flying clouds, betinged with ruddy light,
   Doth on the brindling wolf and wood-boar shine;
When even-star, fair herald of the night,
   Spreads the dark dusky sheen along the mees,
The writhing adders sends a gloomy light,
   And owlets wing from lightning-blasted trees;
Arise, my sprite, and seek the distant dell,
And there to echoing tongues thy raptured joys y-tell.

★ ★ ★ ★ ★

When spring came dancing on a floweret bed,
   Dight in green raiment of a changing kind,
The leaves of hawthorn budding on his head,
   And white primroses cowering to the wind,
Then did the shepherd his long alban spread
   Upon the greeny bank, and danced around,
Whilst the soft flowerets nodded on his head,
   And his fair lambs besprengèd on the ground;
Aneath his foot the brooklets ran along,
Which strollèd round the vale to hear his joyous song.

THOMAS CHATTERTON (1752–1770)

Neap Tide

From: The Borough

When tides were neap, and, in the sultry day,
Through the tall bounding mud-banks made their way,
Which on each side rose swelling, and below
The dark warm flood ran silently and slow;
There anchoring, Peter chose from man to hide,
There hang his head, and view the lazy tide
In its hot slimy channel slowly glide;
Where the small eels that left the deeper way
For the warm shore, within the shallows play;
Where gaping muscles, left upon the mud,
Slope their slow passage to the fallen flood;—
Here dull and hopeless he'd lie down and trace
How sidelong crabs had scrawl'd their crooked race,
Or sadly listen to the tuneless cry
Of fishing gull or clanging golden-eye;
What time the sea-birds to the marsh would come,
And the loud bittern, from the bull-rush home,
Gave from the salt ditch side the bellowing boom:
He nursed the feelings these dull scenes produce,
And loved to stop beside the opening sluice;
Where the small stream, confined in narrow bound,
Ran with a dull, unvaried, sadd'ning sound;
Where all, presented to the eye or ear,
Oppress'd the soul with misery, grief, and fear.

GEORGE CRABBE (1754-1832)

The Sea near Brighton. *John Constable*

Summer Sea
From: *The Borough*

Then the broad bosom of the ocean keeps
An equal motion; swelling as it sleeps,
Then slowly sinking; curling to the strand,
Faint, lazy waves o'ercreep the rigid sand,
Or tap the tarry boat with gentle blow,
And back return in silence, smooth and slow.

GEORGE CRABBE (1754–1832)

Seashore
From: The Borough

Now is it pleasant in the summer-eve,
When a broad shore retiring waters leave,
Awhile to wait upon the firm fair sand,
When all is calm at sea, all still at land;
And there the ocean's produce to explore,
As floating by, or rolling on the shore;
Those living jellies which the flesh inflame,
Fierce as a nettle, and from that its name;
Some in huge masses, some that you may bring
In the small compass of a lady's ring;
Figured by hand divine—there's not a gem
Wrought by man's art to be compared to them;
Soft, brilliant, tender, through the wave they glow,
And make the moonbeam brighter where they flow.
Involved in sea-wrack, here you find a race,
Which science doubting, knows not where to place;
On shell or stone is dropp'd the embryo-seed,
And quicky vegetates a vital breed.
    While thus with pleasing wonder you inspect
Treasures the vulgar in their scorn reject,
See as they float along th' entangled weeds
Slowly approach, upborne on bladdery beads;
Wait till they land, and you shall then behold
The fiery sparks those tangled fronds infold,
Myriads of living points; th' unaided eye
Can but the fire and not the form descry.

And now your view upon the ocean turn,
And there the splendour of the waves discern;
Cast but a stone, or strike them with an oar,
And you shall flames within the deep explore;
Or scoop the stream phosphoric as you stand,
And the cold flames shall flash along your hand;
When, lost in wonder, you shall walk and gaze
On weeds that sparkle, and on waves that blaze.
The ocean too has winter-views serene,
When all you see through densest fog is seen;
When you can hear the fishers near at hand
Distinctly speak, yet see not where they stand;
Or sometimes them and not their boat discern,
Or half-conceal'd some figure at the stern;
The view's all bounded, and from side to side
Your utmost prospect but a few ells wide;
Boys who, on shore, to sea the pebble cast,
Will hear it strike against the viewless mast;
While the stern boatman growls his fierce disdain,
At whom he knows not, whom he threats in vain.

GEORGE CRABBE (1754-1832)

Coast Scene. *George Barret Junior*

To the Evening Star

Thou fair-hair'd angel of the evening,
Now, while the sun rests on the mountains, light
Thy bright torch of love; thy radiant crown
Put on, and smile upon our evening bed!
Smile on our loves, and while thou drawest the
Blue curtains of the sky, scatter thy silver dew
On every flower that shuts its sweet eyes
In timely sleep. Let thy west wind sleep on
The lake; speak silence with thy glimmering eyes,
And wash the dusk with silver. Soon, full soon,
Dost thou withdraw; then the wolf rages wide,
And the lion glares thro' the dun forest:
The fleeces of thy flocks are cover'd with
Thy sacred dew: protect them with thine influence.

WILLIAM BLAKE (1757-1827)

Auguries of Innocence

To see a World in a grain of sand,
And a Heaven in a wild flower,
Hold Infinity in the palm of your hand,
And Eternity in an hour.
A robin redbreast in a cage
Puts all Heaven in a rage.
A dove-house fill'd with doves and pigeons
Shudders Hell thro' all its regions.
A dog starv'd at his master's gate
Predicts the ruin of the State.
A horse misus'd upon the road
Calls to Heaven for human blood.
Each outcry of the hunted hare
A fibre from the brain does tear.

A skylark wounded in the wing,
A cherubim does cease to sing.
The game-cock clipt and arm'd for fight
Does the rising sun affright.
Every wolf's and lion's howl
Raises from Hell a Human soul.
The wild deer, wandering here and there,
Keeps the Human soul from care.
The lamb misus'd breeds public strife,
And yet forgives the butcher's knife.
He who shall hurt the little wren
Shall never be belov'd by men.
He who the ox to wrath has mov'd
Shall never be by woman lov'd.
The wanton boy that kills the fly
Shall feel the spider's enmity.
He who torments the chafer's sprite
Weaves a bower in endless night.
The caterpillar on the leaf
Repeats to thee thy mother's grief.
Kill not the moth nor butterfly,
For the Last Judgement draweth nigh.
He who shall train the horse to war
Shall never pass the polar bar.
The beggar's dog and widow's cat,
Feed them, and thou wilt grow fat.
The bat that flits at close of eve
Has left the brain that won't believe.
The owl that calls upon the night
Speaks the unbeliever's fright.
The gnat that sings his summer's song
Poison gets from Slander's tongue.
The poison of the snake and newt
Is the sweat of Envy's foot.
The poison of the honey-bee
Is the artist's jealousy.
A truth that's told with bad intent
Beats all the lies you can invent.

WILLIAM BLAKE (1757-1827)

Song of Spring

From: Milton

Thou hearest the Nightingale begin the Song of Spring:
The Lark, sitting upon his earthy bed, just as the morn
Appears, listens silent; then, springing from the waving
    cornfield, loud
He leads the Choir of Day—trill! trill! trill! trill!
Mounting upon the wings of light into the great Expanse,
Re-echoing against the lovely blue and shining heavenly
    Shell;
His little throat labours with inspiration; every feather
On throat and breast and wings vibrates with the effluence
    Divine.
All Nature listens silent to him, and the awful Sun
Stands still upon the mountain looking on this little Bird
With eyes of soft humility and wonder, love and awe.
Then loud from their green covert all the Birds begin their
    song:
The Thrush, the Linnet and the Goldfinch, Robin and the
    Wren
Awake the Sun from his sweet revery upon the mountain:
The Nightingale again assays his song, and thro' the day
And thro' the night warbles luxuriant; every Bird of song
Attending his loud harmony with admiration and love.
This is a Vision of the lamentation of Beulah over Ololon.
Thou perceivest the Flowers put forth their precious
    Odours;

And none can tell how from so small a centre comes such
  sweet,
Forgetting that within that centre Eternity expands
Its ever-during doors, that Og and Anak fiercely guard.
First, ere the morning breaks, joy opens in the flowery
  bosoms,
Joy even to tears, which the Sun rising dries: first the Wild
  Thyme
And Meadow-sweet, downy and soft, waving among the
  reeds,
Light springing on the air, lead the sweet dance; they
  wake
The Honeysuckle sleeping on the oak; the flaunting
  beauty
Revels along upon the wind; the White-thorn, lovely
  May,
Opens her many lovely eyes; listening the Rose still
  sleeps—
None dare to wake her; soon she bursts her
  crimson-curtain'd bed
And comes forth in the majesty of beauty. Every Flower,
The Pink, the Jessamine, the Wallflower, the Carnation,
The Jonquil, the mild Lily opes her heavens; every tree
And Flower and Herb soon fill the air with an
  innumerable dance,
Yet all in order sweet and lovely. Men are sick with love!

WILLIAM BLAKE (1757-1827)

The Primrose

Dost ask me, why I send thee here,
This firstling of the infant year—
This lovely native of the vale,
That hangs so pensive and so pale?

Look on its bending stalk, so weak
That, each way yielding, doth not break,
And see how aptly it reveals
The doubts and fears a lover feels.

Look on its leaves of yellow hue
Bepearl'd thus with morning dew,
And these will whisper in thine ears
'The sweets of love are wash'd with tears.'

ROBERT BURNS (1759-1796)

Ye Flowery Banks

Ye flowery banks o' bonie Doon,
   How can ye blume sae fair?
How can ye chant, ye little birds,
   And I sae fu' o' care?

Thou'll break my heart, thou bonie bird
   That sings upon the bough:
Thou minds me o' the happy days
   When my fause luve was true.

Thou'll break my heart, thou bonie bird
   That sings beside thy mate;
For sae I sat, and sae I sang,
   And wist na o' my fate.

Aft hae I rov'd by bonie Doon,
   To see the woodbine twine,
And ilka bird sang o' its luve,
   And sae did I o' mine.

Wi' lightsome heart I pu'd a rose,
   Frae aff its thorny tree;
And my fause luver staw may rose,
   But left the thorn wi' me.

ROBERT BURNS (1759–1796)

Now Spring Has Clad The Grove in Green

Now spring has clad the grove in green
    And strewed the lea wi' flowers:
The furrow'd, waving corn is seen
    Rejoice in fostering showers.
While ilka thing in Nature join
    Their sorrows to forego,
O why thus all alone are mine
    The weary steps o' woe.

The trout within yon wimpling burn
    That glides—a silver dart,
And safe beneath the shady thorn
    Defies the angler's art:
My life was ance that careless stream,
    That wanton trout was I;
But Love, wi' unrelenting beam,
    Has scorch'd my fountains dry.

The little floweret's peaceful lot
 In yonder cliff that grows—
Which, save the linnet's flight, I wot,
 Nae ruder visit knows—
Was mine; till Love has o'er me past
 And blighted a' my bloom,
And now beneath the withering blast
 My youth and joy consume.

The waken'd lav'rock warbling springs,
 And climbs the early sky,
Winnowing blythe her dewy wings
 In morning's rosy eye;
As little reckt I sorrow's power,
 Until the flowery snare
Of witching love, in luckless hour,
 Made me the thrall o' care.

O had my fate been Greenland snows,
 Or Afric's burning zone,
Wi' man and nature leagu'd my foes,
 So Peggy ne'er I'd known!
The wretch whase doom is, 'hope nae mair,'
 What tongue his woes can tell;
Within whase bosom save Despair
 Nae kinder spirits dwell.

ROBERT BURNS (1759-1796)

Bamborough Castle

Ye holy towers that shade the wave-worn steep,
Long may ye rear your aged brows sublime,
Though, hurrying silent by, relentless Time
Assail you, and the winds of winter sweep
Round your dark battlements; for far from halls
Of pride, here Charity hath fixed her seat,
Oft listening, tearful, when the tempests beat
With hollow bodings round your ancient walls;
And Pity, at the dark and stormy hour
Of midnight, when the moon is hid on high,
Keeps   her lone watch upon the topmost tower,
And turns her ear to each expiring cry;
Blessed if her aid some fainting wretch may save,
And snatch him cold and speechless from the wave.

WILLIAM LISLE BOWLES (1762-1850)

Bamborough Castle. *Thomas Girtin*

Fonthill Abbey. *J.C. Buckler*

Fonthill Abbey

The mighty master waved his wand, and, lo!
On the astonished eye the glorious show
Burst like a vision! Spirit of the place!
Has the Arabian wizard with his mace
Smitten the barren downs, far onward spread,
And bade the enchanted palace rise instead?
Bade the dark woods their solemn shades extend
High to the clouds yon spiry tower ascend?
And starting from the umbrageous avenue
Spread the rich pile, magnificent to view?
Enter! from the arched portal look again
Back on the lessening woods and distant plain!
Ascend the steps! the high and fretted roof
Is woven by some elfin hand aloof:
Whilst from the painted windows' long array
A mellow light is shed as not of day.
How gorgeous all! O, never may the spell
Be broken that arrayed those radiant forms so well!

WILLIAM LISLE BOWLES (1762–1850)

38

Lines

Composed a few miles above Tintern Abbey, on revisiting the banks of the Wye during a tour. July 13, 1798

Five years have past; five summers, with the length
Of five long winters! and again I hear
These waters, rolling from their mountain-springs
With a sweet inland murmur.—Once again
Do I behold these steep and lofty cliffs,
That on a wild secluded scene impress
Thoughts of more deep seclusion; and connect
The landscape with the quiet of the sky.
The day is come when I again repose
Here, under this dark sycamore, and view
These plots of cottage-ground, these orchard-tufts,
Which at this season, with their unripe fruits,
Are clad in one green hue, and lose themselves
Among the woods and copses, nor disturb
The wild green landscape. Once again I see
These hedge-rows, hardly hedge-rows, little lines
Of sportive wood run wild; and wreaths of smoke
Sent up, in silence, from among the trees:
With some uncertain notice, as might seem
Of vagrant dwellers in the houseless woods,
Or of some Hermit's cave, where by his fire
The Hermit sits alone.

These beauteous forms,
Through a long absence, have not been to me
As is a landscape to a blind man's eye:
But oft, in lonely rooms, and 'mid the din
Of towns and cities, I have owed to them,
In hours of weariness, sensations sweet,
Felt in the blood, and felt along the heart;
And passing even into my purer mind,
With tranquil restoration:—feelings too
Of unremembered pleasure: such, perhaps,
As have no slight or trivial influence
On that best portion of a good man's life,
His little, nameless, unremembered acts
Of kindness and of love. Nor less, I trust,
To them I may have owed another gift,
Of aspect more sublime; that blessed mood,
In which the burthen of the mystery,
In which the heavy and the weary weight
Of all this unintelligible world,
Is lightened:—that serene and blessed mood,
In which the affections gently lead us on,—
Until, the breath of this corporeal frame
And even the motion of our human blood
Almost suspended, we are laid asleep
In body, and become a living soul:
While with an eye made quiet by the power
Of harmony, and the deep power of joy,
We see into the life of things.

                    If this
Be but a vain belief, yet, oh! how oft—
In darkness and amid the many shapes
Of joyless daylight; when the fretful stir
Unprofitable, and the fever of the world,
Have hung upon the beatings of my heart—
How oft, in spirit, have I turned to thee,
O sylvan Wye! Thou wanderer thro' the woods,
How often has my spirit turned to thee!

    And now, with gleams of half-extinguished thought,
With many recognitions dim and faint,
And somewhat of a sad perplexity,
The picture of the mind revives again:
While here I stand, not only with the sense
Of present pleasure, but with pleasing thoughts
That in this moment there is life and food
For future years. And so I dare to hope,
Though changed, no doubt, from what I was when first
I came among these hills; when like a roe
I bounded o'er the mountains, by the sides
Of the deep rivers, and the lonely streams,
Wherever nature led: more like a man
Flying from something that he dreads, than one
Who sought the thing he loved. For nature then
(The coarser pleasures of my boyish days,
And their glad animal movements all gone by)
To me was all in all.—I cannot paint
What then I was. The sounding cataract
Haunted me like a passion: the tall rock,

The mountain, and the deep and gloomy wood,
Their colours and their forms, were then to me
An appetite; a feeling and a love,
That had no need of a remoter charm,
By thought supplied, nor any interest
Unborrowed from the eye.—That time is past,
And all its aching joys are now no more,
And all its dizzy raptures. Not for this
Faint I, nor mourn nor murmur; other gifts
Have followed; for such loss, I would believe,
Abundant recompence. For I have learned
To look on nature, not as in the hour
Of thoughtless youth; but hearing oftentimes
The still, sad music of humanity,
Nor harsh nor grating, though of ample power
To chasten and subdue. And I have felt
A presence that disturbs me with the joy
Of elevated thoughts; a sense sublime
Of something far more deeply interfused,
Whose dwelling is the light of setting suns,
And the round ocean and the living air,
And the blue sky, and in the mind of man;
A motion and a spirit, that impels
All thinking things, all objects of all thought,
And rolls through all things. Therefore am I still
A lover of the meadows and the woods,
And mountains; and of all that we behold
From this green earth; of all the mighty world
Of eye, and ear,—both what they half create,
And what perceive; well pleased to recognise
In nature and the language of the sense,
The anchor of my purest thoughts, the nurse,
The guide, the guardian of my heart, and the soul
Of all my moral being.

Tintern Abbey. *John Crome*

                              Nor perchance,
If I were not thus taught, should I the more
Suffer my genial spirits to decay:
For thou art with me here upon the banks
Of this fair river; thou my dearest Friend,
My dear, dear Friend; and in thy voice I catch
The language of my former heart, and read
My former pleasures in the shooting lights
Of thy wild eyes. Oh! yet a little while
May I behold in thee what I was once,
My dear, dear Sister! and this prayer I make,
Knowing that Nature never did betray,
The heart that loved her; 'tis her privilege,
Through all the years of this our life, to lead
From joy to joy: for she can so inform
The mind that is within us, so impress
With quietness and beauty, and so feed
With lofty thoughts, that neither evil tongues,
Rash judgments, nor the sneers of selfish men,
Nor greetings where no kindness is, nor all
The dreary intercourse of daily life,
Shall e'er prevail against us, or disturb
Our cheerful faith, that all which we behold
Is full of blessings. Therefore let the moon
Shine on thee in thy solitary walk;

And let the misty mountain-winds be free
To blow against thee: and, in after years,
When these wild ecstasies shall be matured
Into a sober pleasure; when thy mind
Shall be a mansion for all lovely forms,
Thy memory be as a dwelling-place
For all sweet sounds and harmonies; oh! then,
If solitude, or fear, or pain, or grief,
Should be thy portion, with what healing thoughts
Of tender joy wilt thou remember me,
And these my exhortations! Nor, perchance—
If I should be where I no more can hear
Thy voice, nor catch from thy wild eyes these gleams
Of past existence—wilt thou then forget
That on the banks of this delightful stream
We stood together; and that I, so long
A worshipper of Nature, hither came
Unwearied in that service: rather say
With warmer love—oh! with far deeper zeal
Of holier love. Nor wilt thou then forget,
That after many wanderings, many years
Of absence, these steep woods and lofty cliffs,
And this green pastoral landscape, were to me
More dear, both for themselves and for thy sake!

WILLIAM WORDSWORTH (1770-1850)

Gordale

At early dawn, or rather when the air
Glimmers with fading light, and shadowy Eve
Is busiest to confer and to bereave;
Then, pensive Votary! let thy feet repair
To Gordale-chasm, terrific as the lair
Where the young lions couch; for so, by leave
Of the propitious hour, thou may'st perceive
The local Deity, with oozy hair
And mineral crown, beside his jaggèd urn,
Recumbent: Him thou may'st behold, who hides
His lineaments by day, yet there presides,
Teaching the docile waters how to turn,
Or (if need be) impediment to spurn,
And force their passage to the salt-sea tides!

WILLIAM WORDSWORTH (1770-1850)

Inside of King's College Chapel, Cambridge

Tax not the royal Saint with vain expense,
With ill-matched aims the Architect who planned—
Albeit labouring for a scanty band
Of white-robed Scholars only—this immense
And glorious Work of fine intelligence!
Give all thou canst; high Heaven rejects the lore
Of nicely-calculated less or more;

So deemed the man who fashioned for the sense
These lofty pillars, spread that branching roof
Self-poised, and scooped into ten thousand cells,
Where light and shade repose, where music dwells
Lingering—and wandering on as loth to die;
Like thoughts whose very sweetness yieldeth proof
That they were born for immortality.

WILLIAM WORDSWORTH (1770-1850)

From: Staffa, the Island

Thanks for the lessons of this spot,—fit school
For the presumptuous thoughts that would assign
Mechanic laws to agency divine;
And, measuring heaven by earth, would overrule
Infinite Power. The pillared vestibule,
Expanding yet precise, the roof embowed,
Might seem designed to humble man, when proud
Of his best workmanship by plan and tool.
Down-bearing with his whole Atlantic weight
Of tide and tempest on that structure's base,
And flashing to that structure's topmost height,
Ocean has proved its strength, and of its grace
In calms is conscious, finding for his freight
Of softest music some responsive place.

WILLIAM WORDWORTH (1770-1850)

My Romantic Theme
From: Marmion

Like April morning clouds, that pass,
With varying shadow, o'er the grass,
And imitate, on field and furrow,
Life's chequer'd scene of joy and sorrow;
Like streamlet of the mountain north,
Now in a torrent racing forth,
Now winding slow its silver train,
And almost slumbering on the plain;
Like breezes of the autumn day,
Whose voice inconstant dies away,
And ever swells again as fast,
When the ear deems its murmur past;
Thus various, my romantic theme
Flits, winds, or sinks, a morning dream.
Yet pleas'd, our eye pursues the trace
Of Light and Shade's inconstant race;
Pleas'd, views the rivulet afar,
Weaving its maze irregular;
And pleas'd, we listen as the breeze
Heaves its wild sigh through autumn trees:
Then, wild as cloud, or stream, or gale,
Flow on, flow unconfin'd, my Tale!

SIR WALTER SCOTT (1771-1832)

November

From: Marmion

November's sky is chill and drear,
November's leaf is red and sear;
Late, gazing down the steepy linn,
That hems our little garden in,
Low in its dark and narrow glen
You scarce the rivulet might ken,
So thick the tangled greenwood grew,
So feeble trill'd the streamlet through:
Now, murmuring hoarse, and frequent seen
Through bush and brier, no longer green,
An angry brook, it sweeps the glade,
Brawls over rock and wild cascade,
And, foaming brown with doubled speed,
Hurries its waters to the Tweed.

   No longer Autumn's glowing red
Upon our Forest hills is shed;
No more beneath the evening beam
Fair Tweed reflects their purple gleam;
Away hath pass'd the heather-bell
That bloom'd so rich on Needpath-fell;
Sallow his brow; and russet bare
Are now the sister-heights of Yair.
The sheep, before the pinching heaven,
To shelter'd dale and down are driven,
Where yet some faded herbage pines,
And yet a watery sunbeam shines:
In meek despondency they eye
The wither'd sward and wintry sky,
And far beneath their summer hill,
Stray sadly by Glenkinnon's rill.

SIR WALTER SCOTT (1771-1832)

Written on the First of December [1793]

Though now no more the musing ear
Delights to listen to the breeze,
That lingers o'er the green-wood shade
  I love thee, Winter! well.

Sweet are the harmonies of Spring,
Sweet is the Summer's evening gale,
And sweet the Autumnal winds that shake
The many-coloured grove.

And pleasant to the sobered soul
The silence of the wintry scene,
When Nature shrouds herself, entranced
  In deep tranquillity.

Not undelightful now to roam
The wild heath sparkling on the sight;
Not undelightful now to pace
  The forest's ample rounds;

And see the spangled branches shine;
And mark the moss of many a hue
That varies the old tree's brown bark,
  Or o'er the grey stone spreads.

And see the clustered berries bright
Amid the holly's gay green leaves;
The ivy round the leafless oak
  That clasps its foliage close.

So Virtue diffident of strength
Clings to Religion's former aid;
So by Religion's aim upheld,
　　Endures calamity.

Nor void of beauties now the spring,
Whose waters hid from summer-sun
Have soothed the thirsty pilgrim's ear
　　With more than melody.

Green moss shines there with ice incased:
The long grass bends its spear-like form:
And lovely is the silvery scene
　　When faint the sun-beams smile.

Reflection too may love the hour
When Nature, hid in Winter's grave,
No more expands the bursting bud,
　　Or bids the flowret bloom;

For Nature soon in Spring's best charms,
Shall rise revived from Winter's grave,
Expand the bursting bud again,
　　And bid the flower re-bloom.

ROBERT SOUTHEY (1774-1843)

Autumnal Song

Very true, the linnets sing
Sweetest in the leaves of spring:
You have found in all these leaves
That which changes and deceives,
And, to pine by sun or star,
Left them, false ones as they are.
But there be who walk beside
Autumn's, till they all have died,
And who lend a patient ear
To low notes from branches sere.

W. S. LANDOR (1775-1864)

Written on the Banks of Wastwater During a Calm

Is this the Lake, the cradle of the storms,
Where silence never tames the mountain-roar,
Where poets fear their self-created forms,
Or sunk in trance severe, their God adore?
Is this the Lake, for ever dark and loud
With wave and tempest, cataract and cloud?
Wondrous, O Nature! is thy sovereign power,
That gives to horror hours of peaceful mirth;
For here might beauty build her summer-bower!
Lo! where yon rainbow spans the smiling earth,
And, clothed in glory, through a silent shower
The mighty Sun comes forth, a godlike birth;
While, 'neath his loving eye, the gentle Lake
Lies like a sleeping child too blest to wake!

JOHN WILSON (1785-1854)

Cambridge. *J. Walker and Edward Burney*

Written at Cambridge

I was not train'd in Academic bowers,
And to those learned streams I nothing owe
Which copious from those twin fair founts do flow;
Mine have been any thing but studious hours.
Yet can I fancy, wandering 'mid thy towers,
Myself a nursling, Granta, of thy lap;
My brow seems tightening with the Doctor's cap,
And I walk *gowned;* feel unusual powers.
Strange forms of logic clothe my admiring speech,
Old Ramus' ghost is busy at my brain;
And my scull teems with notions infinite.
Be still, ye reeds of Camus, while I teach
Truths, which transcend the searching Schoolmen's vein,
And half had stagger'd that stout Stagirite!

CHARLES LAMB (1775–1834)

53

'Oft, in the Stilly Night'

Oft, in the stilly night,
Ere Slumber's chain has bound me,
Fond Memory brings the light
  Of other days around me;
    The smiles, the tears,
    Of boyhood's years,
  The words of love then spoken;
    The eyes that shone,
    Now dimm'd and gone,
  The cheerful hearts now broken!
Thus, in the stilly night,
  Ere Slumber's chain hath bound me,
Sad Memory brings the light
  Of other days around me.

When I remember all
  The friends, so link'd together,
I've seen around me fall,
  Like leaves in wintry weather;
    I feel like one,
    Who treads alone
  Some banquet-hall deserted,
    Whose lights are fled,
    Whose garlands dead,
  And all but he departed!
Thus, in the stilly night,
  Ere Slumber's chain has bound me,
Sad Memory brings the light
  Of other days around me.

THOMAS MOORE (1779-1852)

The Grasshopper and the Cricket

Green little vaulter in the sunny grass,
  Catching your heart up at the feel of June,
  Sole voice that's heard amidst the lazy noon,
When even the bees lag at the summoning brass;—
And you, warm little housekeeper, who class
  With those who think the candles come too soon,
  Loving the fire, and with your tricksome tune
Nick the glad silent moments as they pass;—

O sweet and tiny cousins, that belong,
  One to the fields, the other to the hearth,
Both have your sunshine; both, though small, are strong
  At your clear hearts; and both seem given to earth
To sing in thoughtful ears this natural song—
  Indoors and out,—summer and winter,—Mirth.

LEIGH HUNT (1784-1859)

The Last Man

All wordly shapes shall melt in gloom,
    The Sun himself must die,
Before this mortal shall assume
    Its Immortality!
I saw a vision in my sleep,
That gave my spirit strength to sweep
    Adown the gulph of Time!
I saw the last of human mould,
That shall Creation's death behold.
    As Adam saw her prime!

The Last Man. *John Martin*

The Sun's eye had a sickly glare,
   The Earth with age was wan,
The skeletons of nations were
   Around that lonely man!
Some had expired in fight,—the brands
Still rested in their bony hands;
   In plague and famine some!
Earth's cities had no sound nor tread;
And ships were drifting with the dead
   To shores where all was dumb!

Yet, prophet-like, that lone one stood
   With dauntless words and high,
That shook the sere leaves from the wood
   As if a storm passed by,
Saying, 'We are twins in death, proud Sun,
Thy face is cold, thy race is run,
   'Tis Mercy bids thee go.
For thou ten thousand thousand years
Hast seen the tide of human tears,
   That shall no longer flow.

'What though beneath thee man put forth
   His pomp, his pride, his skill;
And arts that made fire, flood, and earth,
   The vassals of his will;—
Yet mourn I not thy parted sway,
Thou dim discrownèd king of day:
   For all those trophied arts
And triumphs that beneath thee sprang,
Healed not a passion or a pang
   Entailed on human hearts.

'Go, let oblivion's curtain fall
   Upon the stage of man,
Nor with thy rising beams recall
   Life's tragedy again.
Its piteous pageants bring not back,
Nor waken flesh, upon the rack
   Of pain anew to writhe;
Stretched in disease's shapes abhorred,
Or mown in battle by the sword,
   Like grass beneath the scythe.

'E'en I am weary in yon skies
    To watch thy fading fire;
Test of all sumless agonies,
    Behold not me expire.
My lips that speak thy dirge of death—
Their rounded gasp and gurgling breath
    To see thou shalt not boast.
The eclipse of Nature spreads my pall,—
The majesty of Darkness shall
    Receive my parting ghost!

'This spirit shall return to Him
    That gave its heavenly spark;
Yet think not, Sun, it shall be dim
    When thou thyself art dark!
No! it shall live again, and shine
In bliss unknown to beams of thine,
    By Him recalled to breath,
Who captive led captivity.
Who robbed the grave of Victory,—
    And took the sting from Death!

'Go, Sun, while Mercy holds me up
    On Nature's awful waste
To drink this last and bitter cup
    Of grief that man shall taste—
Go, tell the night that hides thy face,
Thou saw'st the last of Adam's race,
    On Earth's sepulchral clod,
The darkening universe defy
To quench his Immortality,
    Or shake his trust in God!'

THOMAS CAMPBELL (1777-1844)

From: America, a Prophecy

Thus wept the Angel voice, & as he wept, the terrible
    blasts
Of trumpets blew a loud alarm across the Atlantic deep.
No trumpets answer; no reply of clarions or of fifes:
Silent the Colonies remain and refuse the loud alarm.

On those vast shady hills between America & Albion's
    shore,
Now barr'd out by the Atlantic sea, call'd Atlantean hills,
Because from their bright summits you may pass to the
    Golden world,
An ancient palace, archetype of mighty Emperies,
Rears its immortal pinnacles, built in the forest of God
By Ariston, the king of beauty, for his stolen bride.

Here on their magic seats the thirteen Angels sat
    perturb'd,
For clouds from the Atlantic hover o'er the solemn roof.

WILLIAM BLAKE (1757–1827)

'Thus wept the Angel voice.' *William Blake*

The Source of the Arveiron. *Francis Towne*

From: *Hymn before Sun-rise, in the Vale of Chamouni*

Hast thou a charm to stay the morning-star
In his steep course? So long he seems to pause
On thy bald awful head, O sovran BLANC,
The Arve and Arveiron at thy base
Rave ceaselessly; but thou, most awful Form!
Risest from forth thy silent sea of pines,
How silently! Around thee and above
Deep is the air and dark, substantial, black,
An ebon mass: methinks thou piercest it,
As with a wedge! But when I look again,
It is thine own calm home, thy crystal shrine,
Thy habitation from eternity!
O dread and silent Mount! I gazed upon thee,
Hence, viper thoughts, that coil around my mind,
      Reality's dark dream!
I turn from you, and listen to the wind,
  Which long has raved unnoticed.
Of agony by torture lengthened out
That lute sent forth! Thou Wind, that rav'st without,
  Bare crag, or mountain-tairn, or blasted tree,
Or pine-grove whither woodman never clomb,
Or lonely house, long held the witches' home,
  Methinks were fitter instruments for thee,
Mad Lutanist! who in this month of showers,
Of dark-brown gardens, and of peeping flowers,
Mak'st Devils' yule, with worse than wintry song,
The blossoms, buds, and timorous leaves among.

SAMUEL TAYLOR COLERIDGE (1772-1834)

The Grove. *John Constable*

A House and Grounds

Were this impossible, I know full well
What sort of house should grace my garden-bell,—
A good, old country lodge, half hid with blooms
Of honied green, and quaint with straggling rooms,
A few of which, white-bedded and well swept,
For friends, whose names endear'd them, should be kept.
Of brick I'd have it, far more broad than high,
With green up to the door, and elm trees nigh;
And the warm sun should have it in his eye.
The tiptoe traveller, peeping through the boughs
O'er my low wall, should bless the pleasant house,
And that my luck might not seem ill-bestow'd,
A bench and spring should greet him on the road.
My grounds should not be large; I like to go
To Nature for a range, and prospect too,
And cannot fancy she'll comprise for me,
Even in a park, her all-sufficiency.
Besides, my thoughts fly far; and when at rest,
Love, not a watch tower, but a lulling nest.
But all the ground I had should keep a look
Of Nature still, have birds'-nests and a brook;
One spot for flowers, the rest all turf and trees;
For I'd not grow my own bad lettuces.
I'd build a walk, however, against rain,
Long, peradventure, as my whole domain,
And so be sure of generous exercise,
The youth of age, and med'cine of the wise.
And this reminds me, that behind some screen
About my grounds, I'd have a bowling-green;
Such as in wits' and merry women's days
Suckling preferred before his walk of bays.
You may still see them, dead as haunts of fairies,
By the old seats of Killigrews and Careys,
Where all, alas, is vanished from the ring,
Wits and black eyes, the skittles and the king!

LEIGH HUNT (1784-1859)

Description of a Summer's Eve

Down the sultry arc of day
The burning wheels have urged their way,
And Eve along the western skies
Spreads her intermingling dyes.
Down the deep, the miry lane,
Creeking comes the empty wain,
And Driver on the shaft-horse sits,
Whistling now and then by fits;
And oft, with his accustom'd call,
Urging on the sluggish Ball.
The barn is still, the master's gone,
And Thresher puts his jacket on,
While Dick, upon the ladder tall,
Nails the dead kite to the wall.
Here comes shepherd Jack at last,
He has penned the sheep-cote fast,
For 'twas but two nights before,
A lamb was eaten on the moor:
His empty wallet *Rover* carries,
Nor for Jack, when near home, tarries.
With lolling tongue he runs to try,
If the horse-trough be not dry.
The milk is settled in the pans,
And supper messes in the cans;
In the hovel carts are wheeled,
And both the colts are drove a-field;
The horses are all bedded up,
And the ewe is with the tup.
The snare for Mister Fox is set,
The leaven laid, the thatching wet,
And Bess has slink'd away to talk
With Roger in the holly-walk.

Now on the settle all, but Bess,
Are set to eat their supper mess;
And Little Tom, and roguish Kate,
Are swinging on the meadow-gate.

Evening. *Samuel Palmer*

Now they chat of various things,
Of taxes, ministers, and kings,
Or else tell all the village news,
How madam did the 'squire refuse;
How parson on his tythes was bent,
And landlord oft distrained for rent.
Thus do they talk, till in the sky
The pale-ey'd moon is mounted high,
And from the alehouse drunken Ned
Had reeled—then hasten all to bed.
The mistress sees that lazy Kate
The happing coal on kitchen grate
Has laid—while master goes throughout,
Sees shutters fast, the mastiff out,
The candles safe, the hearths all clear,
And nought from thieves or fire to fear;
Then both to bed together creep,
And join the general troop of sleep.

HENRY KIRKE WHITE (1785-1806)

The Sun-dial

The ivy o'er the mouldering wall
Spreads like a tree, the growth of years:
The wild wind through the doorless hall
A melancholy music rears,
A solitary voice, that sighs,
O'er man's forgotten pageantries.
   Above the central gate, the clock,
Through clustering ivy dimly seen,
Seems, like the ghost of Time, to mock
The wrecks of power that once has been.
The hands are rusted on its face;
Even where they ceased, in years gone by,
To keep the flying moments' pace;
Fixing, in Fancy's thoughtful eye,
A point of ages passed away,
A speck of time, that owns no tie
With aught that lives and breathes to-day.
   But 'mid the rank and towering grass,
Where breezes wave, in mournful sport,
The weeds that choke the ruined court,
The careless hours, that circling pass,
Still trace upon the dialled brass
The shade of their unvarying way:
And evermore, with every ray
That breaks the clouds and gilds the air,
Time's stealthy steps are imaged there:
Even as the long-revolving years
In self-reflecting circles flow,
From the first bud the hedgerow bears,
To wintry Nature's robe of snow.

The changeful forms of mortal things
Decay and pass; and art and power
Oppose in vain the doom that flings
Oblivion in their closing hour;
While still, to every woodland vale,
New blooms, new fruits, the seasons bring,
For other eyes and lips to hail
With looks and sounds of welcoming:
As where some stream light-eddying roves
By sunny meads and shadowy groves,
Wave following wave departs for ever,
But still flows on the eternal river.

THOMAS LOVE PEACOCK (1785-1866)

Written in July, 1824

How oft amid the heaped and bedded hay,
Under the oak's broad shadow deep and strong,
Have we sate listening to the noonday song
(If song it were, monotonously gay)
Which crept along the field, the summer lay
    Of the grasshopper. Summer is come in pride
    Of fruit and flower, garlanded as a bride,
And crowned with corn, and graced with length of day.
    But cold is come with her. We sit not now
Listening that merry music of the earth
    Like Ariel 'beneath the blossomed bough;'
But all for chillness round the social hearth
We cluster.—Hark!—a note of kindred mirth
    Echoes!—Oh, wintery cricket, welcome thou!

MARY RUSSELL MITFORD (1787-1855)

Kubla Khan

In Xanadu did Kubla Khan
A stately pleasure-dome decree:
Where Alph, the sacred river, ran
Through caverns measureless to man
   Down to a sunless sea.
So twice five miles of fertile ground
With walls and towers were girdled round:
And there were gardens bright with sinuous rills,
Where blossomed many an incense-bearing tree;
And here were forests ancient as the hills,
Enfolding sunny spots of greenery.

But oh! that deep romantic chasm which slanted
Down the green hill athwart a cedarn cover!
A savage place! as holy and enchanted
As e'er beneath a waning moon was haunted
By woman wailing for her demon-lover!
And from this chasm, with ceaseless turmoil seething,
As if this earth in fast thick pants were breathing,
A might fountain momently was forced:
Amid whose swift half-intermitted burst
Huge fragments vaulted like rebounding hail,
Or chaffy grain beneath the thresher's flail:
And 'mid these dancing rocks at once and ever
It flung up momently the sacred river,
Five miles meandering with a mazy motion
Through wood and dale the sacred river ran,
Then reached the caverns measureless to man,
And sank in tumult to a lifeless ocean:
And 'mid this tumult Kubla heard from far
Ancestral voices prophesying war!

The shadow of the dome of pleasure
Floated midway on the waves;
Where was heard the mingled measure
From the fountain and the caves.
It was a miracle of rare device,
A sunny pleasure-dome with caves of ice!

A damsel with a dulcimer
In a vision once I saw:
It was an Abyssinian maid,
And on her dulcimer she played,
Singing of Mount Abora.
Could I revive within me
Her symphony and song,
To such a deep delight 'twould win me,
That with music loud and long,
I would build that dome in air,
That sunny dome! those caves of ice!
And all who heard should see them there,
And all should cry, Beware! Beware!
His flashing eyes, his floating hair!
Weave a circle round him thrice,
And close your eyes with holy dread,
For he on honey-dew hath fed,
And drunk the milk of Paradise.

SAMUEL TAYLOR COLERIDGE (1772-1834)

Norman Abbey

From: Don Juan

To Norman Abbey whirl'd the noble pair,—
   An old, old monastery once, and now
Still older mansion,—of a rich and rare
   Mix'd Gothic, such as artists all allow
Few specimens yet left us can compare
   Withal: it lies perhaps a little low
Because the monks preferr'd a hill behind,
To shelter their devotion from the wind.

It stood embosom'd in a happy valley,
   Crown'd by high woodlands, where the Druid oak
Stood, like Caractacus, in act to rally
   His host, with broad arms 'gainst the thunderstroke,
And from beneath his boughs were seen to sally
   The dappled foresters; as day awoke,
The branching stag swept down with all his herd,
To quaff a brook which murmur'd like a bird.

Before the mansion lay a lucid lake,
   Broad as transparent, deep, and freshly fed
By a river, which its soften'd way did take
   In currents through the calmer water spread
Around: the wildfowl nestled in the brake
   And sedges, brooding in their liquid bed:
The woods sloped downwards to its brink, and stood
With their green faces fix'd upon the flood.

Its outlet dash'd into a deep cascade,
   Sparkling with foam, until again subsiding,
Its shriller echoes—like an infant made
   Quiet—sank into softer ripples, gliding
Into a rivulet: and thus allay'd,
   Pursued its course, now gleaming, and now hiding
Its windings through the woods; now clear, now blue,
According as the skies their shadows threw.

Landscape with Ruins. *Joseph Wright*

A glorious remnant of the Gothic pile
    (While yet the church was Rome's) stood half apart
In a grand arch, which once screen'd many an aisle.
    These last had disappear'd—a loss to art:
The first yet frown'd superbly o'er the soil,
    And kindled feelings in the roughest heart,
Which mourn'd the power of time's or tempest's march,
In gazing on that venerable arch.

Within a niche, nigh to its pinnacle,
    Twelve saints had once stood sanctified in stone;
But these had fallen, not when the friars fell,
    But in the war which struck Charles from his throne,
When each house was a fortalice—as tell
    The annals of full many a line undone,—
The gallant cavaliers, who fought in vain
For those who knew not to resign or reign.

But in a higher niche, alone, but crown'd,
    The Virgin-Mother of the God-born Child,
With her Son in her blessed arms, look'd round;
    Spared by some chance when all beside was spoil'd;
She made the earth below seem holy ground.
    This may be superstition, weak or wild,
But even the faintest relics of a shrine
Of any worship wake some thoughts divine.

A mighty window, hollow in the centre,
    Shorn of its glass of thousand colourings,
Through which the deepen'd glories once could enter,
    Streaming from off the sun like seraph's wings,
Now yawns all desolate: now loud, now fainter,
    The gale sweeps through its fretwork and oft sings
The owl his anthem, where the silenced quire
Lie with their hallelujahs quench'd like fire.

But in the noontide of the moon, and when
　　The wind is wingèd from one point of heaven,
There moans a strange unearthly sound, which then
　　Is musical—a dying accent driven
Through the huge arch, which soars and sinks again.
　　Some deem it but the distant echo given
Back to the night wind by the waterfall,
And harmonised by the old choral wall:

Others, that some original shape, or form
　　Shaped by decay perchance, hath given the power
(Though less than that of Memnon's statue, warm
　　In Egypt's rays, to harp at a fix'd hour)
To this grey ruin, with a voice to charm
　　Sad, but serene, it sweeps o'er tree or tower;
The cause I know not, nor can solve; but such
The fact:—I've heard it,—once perhaps too much.

Amidst the court a Gothic fountain play'd,
　　Symmetrical, but deck'd with carvings quaint—
Strange faces, like to men in masquerade,
　　And here perhaps a monster, there a saint:
The spring gush'd through grim mouths of granite made,
　　And sparkled into basins, where it spent
Its little torrent in a thousand bubbles,
Like man's vain glory, and his vainer troubles.

The mansion's self was vast and venerable,
　　With more of the monastic than has been
Elsewhere preserved: the cloisters still were stable,
　　The cells, too, and refectory, I ween:
An exquisite small chapel had been able,
　　Still unimpair'd, to decorate the scene;
The rest had been reform'd, replaced, or sunk,
And spoke more of the baron than the monk.

Huge halls, long galleries, spacious chambers, join'd
  By no quite lawful marriage of the arts,
Might shock a connoisseur; but when combined,
  Form'd a whole which, irregular in parts,
Yet left a grand impression on the mind,
  At least of those whose eyes are in their hearts:
We gaze upon a giant for his stature,
Nor judge at first if all be true to nature.

Steel barons, molten the next generation
  To silken rows of gay and garter'd earls,
Glanced from the walls in goodly preservation:
  And Lady Marys blooming into girls,
With fair long locks, had also kept their station:
  And countesses mature in robes and pearls:
Also some beauties of Sir Peter Lely,
Whose drapery hints we may admire them freely.

Judges in very formidable ermine
  Were there, with brows that did not much invite
The accused to think their lordships would determine
  His cause by leaning much from might to right:
Bishops, who had not left a single sermon;
  Attorneys-general, awful to the sight,
As hinting more (unless our judgments warp us)
Of the 'Star Chamber' than of 'Habeas Corpus.'

Generals, some all in armour, of the old
  And iron time, ere lead had ta'en the lead;
Others in wigs of Marlborough's martial fold,
  Huger than twelve of our degenerate breed:
Lordlings, with staves of white or keys of gold:
  Nimrods, whose canvas scarce contain'd the steed;
And here and there some stern high patriot stood,
Who could not get the place for which he sued.

LORD BYRON (1788-1824)

Storm. *David Cox*

Stormy Coast
From: Don Juan

It was a wild and breaker-beaten coast,
　With cliffs above, and a broad sandy shore,
Guarded by shoals and rocks as by an host,
　With here and there a creek, whose aspect wore
A better welcome to the tempest tost;
　And rarely ceased the haughty billow's roar,
Save on the dead long summer days, which make
The outstretch'd ocean glitter like a lake.

LORD BYRON (1788-1824)

Stonehenge

From: The Newdigate Prize Poem, 1823

Wrapt in the veil of time's unbroken gloom,
Obscure as death and silent as the tomb,
Where cold oblivion holds her dusky reign,
Frowns the dark pile on Sarum's lonely plain.
  Yet think not here with classic eye to trace
Corinthian beauty or Ionian grace;
No pillared lines with sculptured foliage crowned,
No fluted remnants deck the hallowed ground;
Firm, as implanted by some Titan's might,
Each rugged stone uprears its giant height,
Whence the poised fragment tottering seems to throw
A trembling shadow on the plain below,
  Here oft, when evening sheds her twilight ray,
And gilds with fainter beam departing day,
With breathless gaze, and cheek with terror pale,
The lingering shepherd startles at the tale,
How at deep midnight by the moon's chill glance
Unearthly forms prolong the viewless dance;
While on each whispering breeze that murmurs by,
His busied fancy hears the hollow sigh.
  Rise from thy haunt, dread genius of the clime,
Rise, magic spirit of forgotten time!
  'Tis thine to burst the mantling clouds of age,
And fling new radiance on tradition's page:
See! at thy call from fable's varied store,
In shadowy train the mingled visions pour;
Here wizard Merlin, where the mighty fell,
Waves the dark wand and chants the thrilling spell.
Hark! 'tis the bardic lyre whose harrowing strain
Wakes the rude echoes of the slumbering pain;
Lo! 'tis the Druid pomp, whose lengthening line
In lowliest homage bends before the shrine.

THOMAS STOKES SALMON (1803-1863)

Stonehenge. *John Constable*

The Devil's Bridge, St Gothard. *J.M.W. Turner*

Song of the Alps

By the edge of the chasm is a slippery track,
The torrent beneath, and the mist hanging o'er thee;
The cliffs of the mountain, huge, rugged, and black,
Are frowning like giants before thee;
And wouldst thou not waken the sleeping Lawine,
Walk silent and soft through the deadly ravine.

That bridge with its dizzying, perilous span
Aloft o'er the gulf and its flood suspended,
Think'st thou it was built by the art of man,
By his hand that grim old arch was bended?
Far down in the jaws of the gloomy abyss
The water is boiling and hissing,—forever will hiss.

Four rivers rush down from on high,
Their spring will be hidden forever;
Their course is to all the four points of the sky,
To each point of the sky is a river;
And fast as they start from their old mother's feet,
They dash forth, and no more will they meet.

Two pinnacles rise to the depths of the blue;
Aloft on their white summits glancing,
Bedecked in their garments of golden dew,
The clouds of the sky are dancing;
There threading alone their lightsome maze,
Uplifted apart from all mortals' gaze.

And high on her ever-enduring throne
The queen of the mountains reposes;
Her head serene and azure and lone
A diamond crown encloses;
The sun with his darts shoots round it keen and hot,
He gilds it always, he warms it not.

FRIEDRICH VON SCHILLER
Translated by THOMAS CARLYLE (17951–881)

The Château of Chillon

From: The Prisoner of Chillon

Lake Leman lies by Chillon's walls:
A thousand feet in depth below
Its massy waters meet and flow;
Thus much the fathom-line was sent
From Chillon's snow-white battlement,
    Which round about the wave inthrals:
A double dungeon wall and wave
Have made—and like a living grave
Below the surface of the lake
The dark vault lies wherein we lay,
We heard it ripple night and day;
    Sounding o'er our heads it knock'd;
And I have felt the winter's spray
Wash through the bars when winds were high
And wanton in the happy sky;
    And then the very rock hath rock'd,
    And I have felt it shake, unshock'd,
Because I could have smiled to see
The death that would have set me free.

LORD BYRON (1788-1824)

The Cloud

I bring fresh showers for the thirsting flowers,
  From the seas and the streams;
I bear light shade for the leaves when laid
  In their noonday dreams.
From my wings are shaken the dews that waken
  The sweet buds every one,
When rocked to rest on their mother's breast,
  As she dances about the sun.
I wield the flail of the lashing hail,
  And whiten the green plains under,
And then again I dissolve it in rain,
  And laugh as I pass in thunder.
I sift the snow on the mountains below,
  And their great pines groan aghast;
And all the night 'tis my pillow white,
  While I sleep in the arms of the blast.
Sublime on the towers of my skiey bowers,
  Lightning my pilot sits;
In a cavern under is fettered the thunder,
  It struggles and howls at fits;
Over earth and ocean, with gentle motion,
  This pilot is guiding me,
Lured by the love of the genii that move
  In the depths of the purple sea;
Over the rills, and the crags, and the hills,
  Over the lakes and the plains,
Wherever he dream, under mountain or stream,
  The Spirit he loves remains;
And I all the while bask in Heaven's blue smile,
  Whilst he is dissolving in rains.

PERCY BYSSHE SHELLEY (1792-1822)

Chillon. *John Varley*

83

To the Nile

Month after month the gathered rains descend
Drenching yon secret Aethiopian dells,
And from the desert's ice-girt pinnacles
Where Frost and Heat in strange embraces blend
On Atlas, fields of moist snow half depend.
Girt there with blasts and meteors Tempest dwells
By Nile's aëriel urn, with rapid spells
Urging those waters to their mighty end.
O'er Egypt's land of Memory floods are level
And they are thine, O Nile—and well thou knowest
That soul-sustaining airs and blasts of evil
And fruits and poisons spring where'er thou flowest.
Beware, O Man—for knowledge must to thee,
Like the great flood to Egypt, ever be.

PERCY BYSSHE SHELLEY (1792-1822)

To the Moon

Art thou pale for weariness
Of climbing heaven and gazing on the earth,
    Wandering companionless
Among the stars that have a different birth,—
And ever changing, like a joyless eye
That finds no object worth its constancy?

PERCY BYSSHE SHELLEY (1792-1822)

The Face of the Moon. *John Russell*

'While the Moon Decks Herself'

While the Moon decks herself in Neptune's glass,
And ponders o'er her image in the sea,
Her cloudy locks smoothing from off her face
That she may all as bright as Beauty be!
It is my wont to sit upon the shore
And mark with what an even grace she glides
Her two concurrent paths of azure o'er,
One in the Heavens, the other in the tides:
Now with a transient veil her face she hides,
And Ocean blackens with a human frown;
Now her fine screen of vapor she divides,
And looks with all her light of beauty down!
Her splendid smile, wide-spreading o'er the main,
Brightens the glass she gazes at again!

GEORGE DARLEY (1795-1845)

85

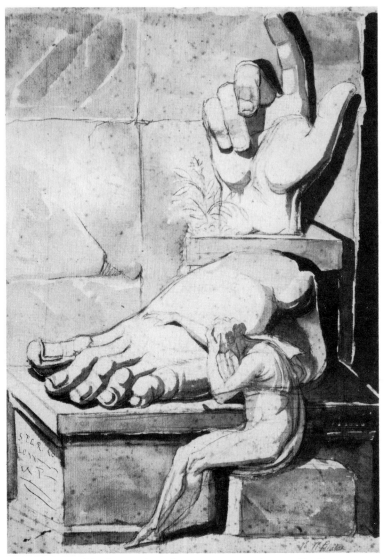

'The Artist moved by the Grandeur of Antique Fragments'. *Henry Fuseli*

Ozymandias

I met a traveller from an antique land
Who said: Two vast and trunkless legs of stone
Stand in the desert. Near them, on the sand,
Half sunk, a shattered visage lies, whose frown,
And wrinkled lip, and sneer of cold command,
Tell that its sculptor well those passions read
Which yet survive, stamped on these lifeless things,
The hand that mocked them, and the heart that fed;
And on the pedestal these words appear:
'My name is Ozymandias, king of kings:
Look on my works, ye Mighty, and despair!'
Nothing beside remains. Round the decay
Of that colossal wreck, boundless and bare
The lone and level sands stretch far away.

PERCY BYSSHE SHELLEY (1792-1822)

Autumn Leaves

From: The Christian Year (1827)

Red o'er the forest peers the setting sun,
  The line of yellow light dies fast away
That crowned the eastern copse: and chill and dun
  Falls on the moor the brief November day.

Now the tired hunter winds a parting note,
  And Echo bids good-night from every glade:
Yet wait awhile, and see the calm leaves float
  Each to his rest beneath their parent shade.

How like decaying life they seem to glide!
  And yet no second spring have they in store,
But where they fall, forgotten to abide
  Is all their portion, and they ask no more.

Soon o'er their heads blithe April airs shall sing,
  A thousand wild-flowers round them shall unfold,
The green buds glisten in the dews of Spring,
  And all be vernal raptures as of old.

Unconscious they in waste oblivion lie,
  In all the world of busy life around
No thought of them; in all the bounteous sky
  No drop, for them, of kindly influence found.

Man's portion is to die and rise again –
  Yet he complains, while these unmurmuring part
With their sweet lives, as pure from sin and stain
  As his when Eden held his virgin heart.

JOHN KEBLE (1792-1866)

Cloud Study. *John Constable*

To the Clouds

O painted clouds! sweet beauties of the sky,
    How have I view'd your motion and your rest,
When like fleet hunters ye have left mine eye,
    In your thin gauze of woolly-fleecing drest;
Or in your threaten'd thunder's grave black vest,
    Like black deep waters slowly moving by,
Awfully striking the spectator's breast
    With your Creator's dread sublimity,
As admiration mutely views your storms.
    And I do love to see you idly lie,
Painted by heav'n as various as your forms,
    Pausing upon the eastern mountain high,
As morn awakes with spring's wood-harmony;
    And sweeter still, when in your slumbers sooth
You hang the western arch o'er day's proud eye:
    Still as the even-pool, uncurv'd and smooth,
My gazing soul has look'd most placidly;
    And higher still devoutly wish'd to strain,
To wipe your shrouds and sky's blue blinders by,
    With all the warmness of a moon-struck brain,—
To catch a glimpse of Him who bids you reign,
    And view the dwelling of all majesty.

JOHN CLARE (1793-1864)

Rain. *David Cox*

Sudden Shower

Black grows the southern sky, betokening rain,
  And humming hive-bees homeward hurry by:
They feel the change; so let us shun the grain,
  And take the broad road while our feet are dry.
Aye there, some drops fell moistening on my face,
  And pattering on my hat—'tis coming nigh!—
Let's look about, and find a sheltering place.
  The little things around us fear the sky,
And hasten through the grass to shun the shower.
  Here stoops an ash-tree—hark! the wind gets high,
But never mind; this ivy, for an hour,
  Rain as it may, will keep us drily here:
That little wren knows well his sheltering bower,
  Nor leaves his covert, though we come so near.

JOHN CLARE (1793-1864)

90

Description of a Thunder-storm

Slow boiling up, on the horizon's brim,
Huge clouds arise, mountainous, dark and grim,
Sluggish and slow upon the air they ride,
As pitch-black ships o'er the blue ocean glide;
Curling and hovering o'er the gloomy south,
As curls the sulphur from the cannon's mouth.
More grizly in the sun the tempest comes,
And through the wood with threatened vengeance hums,
Hissing more loud and loud among the trees:—
The frighted wild-wind trembles to a breeze,
Just turns the leaf in terrifying sighs,
Bows to the spirit of the storm, and dies.
In wild pulsations beats the heart of fear,
At the low rumbling thunder creeping near.
The poplar leaf now resteth on its tree;
And the mill-sail, once twirling rapidly,
Lagging and lagging till each breeze had dropt,
Abruptly now in hesitation stopt.
The very cattle gaze upon the gloom,
And seemly dread the threat'ned fate to come.
The little birds sit mute within the bush,
And nature's very breath is stopt and hush.
The shepherd leaves his unprotected flock,
And flies for shelter in some scooping rock;
There hides in fear from the dread boding wrath,
Lest rocks should tremble when it sallies forth,
And that almighty Power, that bids it roar,
Hath seal'd the doom when time shall be no more.
The cotter's family cringe round the hearth,
Where all is sadden'd but the cricket's mirth:
The boys through fear in soot-black corner push,
And 'tween their father's knees for safety crush;

Each leaves his plaything on the brick-barr'd floor,
The idle top and ball can please no more,
And oft above the wheel's unceasing thrum
The murmur's heard to whisper,—"Is it come!"
The clouds more dismal darken on the eye,
More huge, more fearful, and of deeper dye;
And, as unable to light up the gloom,
The sun drops sinking in its bulging tomb.
Now as one glances sky-ward with affright,
Short vivid lightnings catch upon the sight;
While like to rumbling armies, as it were,
Th'approaching thunder mutters on the ear,
And still keeps creeping on more loud and loud,
And stronger lightnings splinter through the cloud.
An awe-struck monument of hope and fear,
Mute expectation waits the terror near,
That dreadful clap, that terminates suspense,
When ruin meets us or is banish'd hence.
The signal's given in that explosive flash,—
One moment's pause—and then the horrid crash:—

—Almighty, what a shock!—the jostled wrack
  Of nature seems in mingled ruins done;
Astounded echo rives the terrors back,
  And tingles on the ear a dying swoon.
Flash, peal, and flash still rend the melting cloud;
  All nature seems to sigh her race is o'er,
And as she shrinks 'neath chaos' dismal shroud,
  Gives meek consent that suns shall shine no more.
Where is the sinner now, with careless eye,
  Will look, and say that all is chance's whim;
When hell e'en trembles at God's majesty,
  And sullen owns that nought can equal him?
But clouds now melt like mercy into tears,
  And nature's Lord his wrath in kindness stops:
Each trembling cotter now delighted hears
  The rain fall down in heavy-pattering drops.
The sun 'gins tremble through the cloud again,
And a slow murmur wakes the delug'd plain;
A murmur of thanksgiving, mix'd with fear,
For God's great power and our deliverance here.

JOHN CLARE (1793-1864)

Foliage

Come forth, and let us through our hearts receive
The joy of verdure!—see, the honed lime
Showers cool green light o'er banks where wild-flowers
   weave
Thick tapestry; and woodbine tendrils climb
Up the brown oak from buds of moss and thyme.
The rich deep masses of the sycamore
Hang heavy with the fulness of their prime,
And the white poplar, from its foliage hoar,
Scatters forth gleams like moonlight, with each gale
That sweeps the boughs:— the chestnut flowers are past,
The crowning glories of the hawthorn fail,
But arches of sweet eglantine are cast
From every hedge:—Oh! never may we lose,
Dear friend! our fresh delight in simplest nature's hues!

FELICIA DOROTHEA HEMANS (1793-1835)

Nightingale Valley. *Francis Danby*

March

The stormy March is come at last,
   With wind, and cloud, and changing skies;
I hear the rushing of the blast,
   That through the snowy valley flies.

Ah, passing few are they who speak,
   Wild, stormy month! in praise of thee;
Yet, though thy winds are loud and bleak,
   Thou art a welcome month to me.

For thou, to northern lands, again
   The glad and glorious sun dost bring,
And thou hast joined the gentle train
   And wear'st the gentle name of Spring.

And, in thy reign of blast and storm,
   Smiles many a long, bright, sunny day,
When the changed winds are soft and warm,
   And heaven puts on the blue of May.

Then sing aloud the gushing rills
   In joy that they again are free,
And, brightly leaping down the hills,
   Renew their journey to the sea.

The year's departing beauty hides
   Of wintry storms the sullen threat;
But in thy sternest frown abides
   A look of kindly promise yet.

Thou bring'st the hope of those calm skies,
   And that soft time of sunny showers,
When the wide bloom, on earth that lies,
   Seems of a brighter world than ours.

WILLIAM CULLEN BRYANT (1794-1878)

To Ailsa Rock

Hearken, thou craggy ocean pyramid!
  Give answer from thy voice, the sea-fowls' screams!
  When were thy shoulders mantled in huge streams?
When, from the sun, was thy broad forehead hid?
How long is't since the mighty power bid
  Thee heave to airy sleep from fathom dreams?
  Sleep in the lap of thunder or sunbeams,
Or when grey clouds are thy cold coverlid.
Thou answer'st not; for thou art dead asleep;
  Thy life is but two dead eternities—
The last in air, the former in the deep;
  First with the whales, last with the eagle-skies—
Drown'd wast thou till an earthquake made thee steep,
  Another cannot wake thy giant size.

JOHN KEATS (1795-1821)

Ode to a Nightingale

My heart aches, and a drowsy numbness pains
  My sense, as though of hemlock I had drunk,
Or emptied some dull opiate to the drains
  One minute past, and Lethe-wards had sunk:
'Tis not through envy of thy happy lot,
  But being too happy in thine happiness,—
    That thou, light-winged Dryad of the trees,
      In some melodious plot
Of beechen green, and shadows numberless,
  Singest of summer in full-throated ease.

O, for a draught of vintage! that hath been
  Cool'd a long age in the deep-delved earth,
Tasting of Flora and the country green,
  Dance, and Provençal song, and sunburnt mirth!
O for a beaker full of the warm South,
  Full of the true, the blushful Hippocrene,
    With beaded bubbles winking at the brim,
      And purple-stained mouth;
    That I might drink, and leave the world unseen
    And with thee fade away into the forest dim:

Fade far away, dissolve, and quite forget
What thou among the leaves hast never known,
The weariness, the fever, and the fret
Here, where men sit and hear each other groan;
Where palsy shakes a few, sad, last gray hairs,
Where youth grows pale, and spectre-thin, and dies;
Where but to think is to be full of sorow
And leaden-eyed despairs,
Where Beauty cannot keep her lustrous eyes,
Or new Love pine at them beyond to-morrow.

Away! away! for I will fly to thee,
Not charioted by Bacchus and his pards,
But on the viewless wings of Poesy,
Though the dull brain perplexes and retards:
Already with thee! tender is the night,
And haply the Queen-Moon is on her throne,
Cluster'd around by all her starry Fays;
But here there is no light,
Save what from heaven is with the breeezes blown
Through verdurous glooms and winding mossy ways.

I cannot see what flowers are at my feet,
Nor what soft incense hangs upon the boughs,
But, in embalmed darkness, guess each sweet
Wherewith the seasonable month endows
The grass, the thicket, and the fruit-tree wild;
White hawthorn, and the pastoral eglantine;
Fast fading violets cover'd up in leaves;
And mid-May's eldest child,
The coming musk-rose, full of dewy wine,
The murmurous haunt of flies on summer eves.

Darkling I listen; and, for many a time
  I have been half in love with easeful Death,
Call'd him soft names in many a mused rhyme,
  To take into the air my quiet breath;
Now more than ever seems it rich to die,
  To cease upon the midnight with no pain,
    While thou art pouring forth thy soul abroad
      In such an ecstasy!
  Still wouldst thou sing, and I have ears in vain—
    To thy high requiem become a sod.

Thou wast not born for death, immortal Bird!
  No hungry generations tread thee down;
The voice I hear this passing night was heard
  In ancient days by emperor and clown:
Perhaps the self-same song that found a path
  Through the sad heart of Ruth, when, sick for home,
    She stood in tears amid the alien corn;
      The same that oft-times hath
Charm'd magic casements, opening on the foam
  Of perilous seas, in faery lands forlorn.

Forlorn! the very word is like a bell
  To toll me back from thee to my sole self!
Adieu! the fancy cannot cheat so well
  As she is fam'd to do, deceiving elf.
Adieu! adieu! thy plaintive anthem fades
  Past the near meadows, over the still stream,
    Up the hill-side; and now 'tis buried deep
      In the next valley-glades:
  Was it a vision, or a waking dream?
    Fled is that music:— Do I wake or sleep?

JOHN KEATS (1795-1821)

To Autumn

Season of mists and mellow fruitfulness,
　Close bosom-friend of the maturing sun;
Conspiring with him how to load and bless
　With fruit the vines that round the thatch-eves run;
To bend with apples the moss'd cottage-trees,
　And fill all fruit with ripeness to the core;
　　To swell the gourd, and plump the hazel shells
　With a sweet kernel; to set budding more,
And still more, later flowers for the bees,
Until they think warm days will never cease,
　　For Summer has o'er-brimm'd their clammy cells.

Who hath not seen thee oft amid thy store?
　Sometimes whoever seeks abroad may find
Thee sitting careless on a granary floor,
　Thy hair soft-lifted by the winnowing wind;
Or on a half-reap'd furrow sound asleep,
　Drows'd with the fume of poppies, while thy hook
　　Spares the next swatch and all its twined flowers:
And sometimes like a gleaner thou dost keep
　Steady thy laden head across a brook;
　Or by a cyder-press, with patient look,
　　Thou watchest the last oozings hours by hours.

Where are the songs of Spring? Ay, where are they?
    Think not of them, thou hast thy music too,—
While barred clouds bloom the soft-dying day,
    And touch the stubble-plains with rosy hue;
Then in a wailful choir the small gnats mourn
    Among the river sallows, borne aloft
        Or sinking as the light wind lives or dies;
And full-grown lambs loud bleat from hilly bourn;
    Hedge-crickets sing; and now with treble soft
    The red-breast whistles from a garden-croft;
        And gathering swallows twitter in the skies.

JOHN KEATS (1795-1821)

On the Sea

It keeps eternal whisperings around
    Desolate shores, and with its mighty swell
    Gluts twice ten thousand caverns, till the spell
Of Hecate leaves them their old shadowy sound.
Often 'tis in such gentle temper found,
    That scarcely will the very smallest shell
    Be mov'd for days from where it sometime fell,
When last the winds of heaven were unbound.
Oh ye! who have your eye-balls vex'd and tir'd
    Feast them upon the wideness of the sea;
        Oh ye! whose ears are dinn'd with uproar rude,
    Or fed too much with cloying melody—
        Sit ye near some old cavern's mouth, and brood
Until ye start, as if the sea-nymphs quir'd!

JOHN KEATS (1795-1821)

There was a cot . . .

There was a cot, a little rustic home,
Which oft I used to pass in careless youth,
Where a sweet child was growing like a flower
In the high fissure of a mossy crag,
Giving a kind and human loveliness
To bleakest solitude—I know not why
In all my rambles, still my steps were led
To that lone dwelling,—still—if e'er I missed
The little maiden with her sun-burn'd face,
Her rosy face that glowed with summer brown,
Quick glancing through the lattice, my heart sank
And all that day my thoughts were matterless
As if defrauded of their daily bread;
But when she lilted from the lowly door
Tossing her burden of crisp, curly locks
That kept her arms in pretty motion still
To give free prospect to her wild blue eyes,
My soul was glad within me, as the deep
Glows with the young light of the sudden Sun,
For three long years I watch'd her, and she seem'd
To greet my coming as a natural thing,
The punctual quitrent of unfailing time.

HARTLEY COLERIDGE (1796-1849)

Lear

A poor old king, with sorrow for my crown,
Throned upon straw, and mantled with the wind—
For pity, my own tears have made me blind
That I might never see my children's frown;
And, may be, madness, like a friend, has thrown
A folded fillet over my dark mind,
So that unkindly speech may sound for kind—
Albeit I know not.—I am childish grown—
And have not gold to purchase wit withal—
I that have once maintain'd most royal state—
A very bankrupt now that may not call
My child, my child—all beggar'd save in tears,
Wherewith I daily weep an old man's fate,
Foolish—and blind—and overcome with years!

THOMAS HOOD (1799-1845)

(overleaf) Mont Blanc and the Arve. *John Robert Cozens*

Clouds

Onriding slow, at lofty height,
Were clouds in drift along the sky,
Of purple blue, and pink, and white,
In pack and pile, upreaching high,
For ever changing, as they flew,
Their shapes from new again to new.

And some like rocks, and towers of stone,
Or hills, or woods, outreaching wide;
And some like roads, with dust upblown
In glittering whiteness off their side,
Outshining white, again to fade,
In figures made to be unmade.

So things may meet, but never stand,
In life; they may be smiles or tears:
A joy in hope, and one in hand;
Some grounds of grief, and some of fears;
They may be good, or may be ill,
But never long abiding still.

WILLIAM BARNES (1801-1886)

Lines

How lovely is the heaven of this night,
How deadly still its earth. The forest brute
Has crept into his cave, and laid himself
Where sleep has made him harmless like the lamb:
The horrid snake, his venom now forgot,
Is still and innocent as the honied flower
Under his head:— and man, in whom are met
Leopard and snake,—and all the gentleness
And beauty of the young lamb and the bud,
Has let his ghost out, put his thoughts aside
And lent his senses unto death himself;
Whereby the King and beggar all lie down
On straw or purple-tissue, are but bones
And air, and blood, equal to one another
And to the unborn and buried: so we go
Placing ourselves among the unconceived
And the old ghosts, wantonly, smilingly
For sleep is fair and warm.

THOMAS LOVELL BEDDOES (1803-1849)

The New-born Star

The world is born to-day!
   What is the world?—Behold the wonder:
   With a mighty thunder,
'Round the sun, it rolls this way;
And its shadow falls afar
   Over many a star,
And the interstellar vale,
Through which some aged, patient globe,
(Whose gaunt sides no summers robe,)
   Like a prisoner through his grate,
   Shivering in despair doth wait
   For sunbeams broken, old, and pale.

   Bounding, like its own fleet deer
   Down a hill, behold a sphere!
   Now a mountain, tall and wide,
   Hanging weighty on its side
   Pulls its down impetuously;
   Yet the little butterfly,
   Whom the daisy's dew doth glut,
   With his wings' small pages shut,
      Was not stirred.

Now forests fall, like clouds that gather
O'er the plain's unruffled weather:
Burst great rocks, with thunder, out:
Lakes, their plunged feet about,
Round, and smooth, and heaving ever,
An unawakened serpent-river
    Coiled and sleeping.
Silver changes now are creeping
Down the descending summit of the ball:
    Pastures break, and steadfast land
Sinks, melting:—mighty ocean is at hand.—
Space for eternal waves! Be strong and wide,
Thou new-born star! Reflecting all the sky,
And its lone sun, the island-starred tide
    Swells billowing by.
At last the dreadful sea is curled
    Behind the nations. Mark ye now
    The death-intending wrinkles of his brow?
He is the murderous Judas of the world.

THOMAS LOVELL BEDDOES (1803-1849)

Shoreham

And now the trembling light
Glimmers behind the little hills and corn,
Ling'ring as loth to part; yet part thou must
And though than open day far pleasing more
(Ere yet the fields and pearlèd cups of flowers
    Twinkle in the parting light;)
Thee night shall hide, sweet visionary gleam
That softly lookest through the rising dew;
    Till all like silver bright,
    The faithful witness, pure and white,
    Shall look o'er yonder grassy hill,
    At this village, safe and still.
    All is safe and all is still,
    Save what noise the watch-dog makes
    Or the shrill cock the silence breaks.
    Now and then—
    And now and then—
    Hark! Once again,
    The wether's bell
    To us doth tell
Some little stirring in the fold.
Methinks the ling'ring dying ray
Of twilight time, doth seem more fair,
And lights the soul up more than day
When wide-spread sultry sunshines are:
Yet all is right and all most fair,
For thou, dear God, has formèd all;
Thou deckest every little flower,
Thou girdest every planet ball,
And mark'st when sparrows fall.

SAMUEL PALMER (1805-1881)

A Summer Twilight

It is a Summer gloaming, balmy-sweet,
A gloaming brighten'd by an infant moon,
Fraught with the fairest light of middle June;
The lonely garden echoes to my feet,
And hark! O hear I not the gentle dews,
Fretting the silent forest in his sleep?
Or does the stir of housing insects creep
Thus faintly on mine ear? Day's many hues,
Waned with the paling light and are no more,
And none but drowsy pinions beat the air:
The bat is hunting softly by my door,
And, noiseless as the snow-flake, leaves his lair;
O'er the still copses flitting here and there,
Wheeling the self-same circuit o'er and o'er.

CHARLES TENNYSON TURNER (1808-1879)

The City in the Sea

Lo! Death has reared himself a throne
In a strange city lying alone
Far down within the dim West,
Where the good and the bad and the worst and the best
Have gone to their eternal rest.
There shrines and palaces and towers
(Time-eaten towers that tremble not!)
Resemble nothing that is ours.
Around, by lifting winds forgot,
Resignedly beneath the sky
The melancholy waters lie.

No rays from the holy heaven come down
On the long night-time of that town;
But light from out the lurid sea
Streams up the turrets silently—
Gleams up the pinnacles far and free—
Up domes—up spires—up kingly halls—
Up fanes—up Babylon-like walls—
Up shadowy long-forgotten bowers
Of sculptured ivy and stone flowers—
Up many and many a marvellous shrine
Whose wreathéd friezes intertwine
The viol, the violet, and the vine.
Resignedly beneath the sky
The melancholy waters lie.
So blend the turrets and shadows there
That all seem pendulous in air,
While from a proud tower in the town
Death looks gigantically down.

There open fanes and gaping graves
Yawn level with the luminous waves;
But not the riches there that lie
In each idol's diamond eye—
Not the gaily-jewelled dead
Tempt the waters from their bed;
For no ripples curl, alas!
Along that wilderness of glass—
No swellings tell that winds may be
Upon some far-off happier sea—
No heavings hint that winds have been
On seas less hideously serene.

But lo, a stir is in the air!
The wave—there is a movement there!
As if the towers had thrust aside,
In slightly sinking, the dull tide—
As if their tops had feebly given
A void within the filmy Heaven.
The waves have now a redder glow—
The hours are breathing faint and low—
And when, amid no earthly moans,
Down, down that town shall settle hence,
Hell, rising from a thousand thrones,
Shall do it reverence.

EDGAR ALLAN POE (1809-1849).

(overleaf) The Enchanted Castle. Francis Danby

To the Mountains

And when the sun puts out his lamp
We'll sleep serene within the camp,
Trusting to his invet'rate skill
Who leads the stars o'er yonder hill,
Whose discipline doth never cease
To watch the slumberings of peace,
And from the virtuous hold afar
The melancholy din of war.—
For ye our sentries still outlie,
The earth your pallet and your screen the sky.

From steadfastness I will not swerve,
Remembering my sweet reserve.

With all your kindness shown from year to year
Ye do but civil demons still appear;
Still to my mind
Ye are inhuman and unkind,
And bear an untamed aspect to my sight
After the 'civil-suited' night,
As if ye had lain out
Like to the Indian scout
Who lingers in the purlieus of the towns
With unexplored grace and savage frowns.

HENRY DAVID THOREAU (1817–1862)

In Nature's Wonderland. *Thomas Doughty*

My Dream

Hear now a curious dream I dreamed last night
Each word whereof is weighed and sifted truth.

   I stood beside Euphrates while it swelled
Like overflowing Jordan in its youth:
It waxed and coloured sensibly to sight;
Till out of myriad pregnant waves there welled
Young crocodiles, a gaunt blunt-featured crew,
Fresh-hatched perhaps and daubed with birthday dew.
The rest if I should tell, I fear my friend
My closest friend would deem the facts untrue;
And therefore it were wisely left untold;
Yet if you will, why, hear it to the end.

   Each crocodile was girt with massive gold
And polished stones that with their wearers grew:
But one there was who waxed beyond the rest,
Wore kinglier girdle and kingly crown,
Whilst crowns and orbs and sceptres starred his breast.
All gleamed compact and green with scale on scale,
But special burnishment adorned his mail
And special terror weighed upon his frown;
His punier brethren quaked before his tail,
Broad as a rafter, potent as a flail.
So he grew lord and master of his kin:
But who shall tell the tale of all their woes?
An execrable appetite arose,
He battened on them, crunched, and sucked them in.

He knew no law, he feared no binding law,
But ground them with inexorable jaw:
The luscious fat distilled upon his chin,
Exuded from his nostrils and his eyes,
While still like hungry death he fed his maw;
Till every minor crocodile being dead
And buried too, himself gorged to the full,
He slept with breath oppressed and unstrung claw.
Oh marvel passing strange which next I saw:
In sleep he dwindled to the common size,
And all the empire faded from his coat.
Then from far off a wingèd vessel came,
Swift as a swallow subtle as a flame:
I know not what it bore of freight or host,
But while it was as an avenging ghost.
It levelled strong Euphrates in its course;
Supreme yet weightless as an idle mote
It seemed to tame the waters without force
Till not a murmur swelled or billow beat:
Lo, as the purple shadow swept the sands,
The prudent crocodile rose on his feet
And shed appropriate tears and wrung his hands.

What can it mean? you ask. I answer not
For meaning, but myself must echo, What?
And tell it as I saw it on the spot.

CHRISTINA ROSSETTI (1830–1894)

(overleaf) Bushey Churchyard. *William Henry Hunt*

121

Mild the Mist upon the Hill

Mild the mist upon the hill,
Telling not of storms to-morrow;
No; the day has wept its fill,
Spent its store of silent sorrow.

Oh, I'm gone back to the days of youth,
I am a child once more;
And 'neath my father's sheltering roof,
And near the old hall door,

I watch this cloudy evening fall,
After a day of rain:
Blue mists, sweet mists of summer pall
The horizon's mountain-chain.

The damp stands in the long, green grass
As thick as morning's tears;
And dreamy scents of fragrance pass
That breathe of other years.

EMILY BRONTË (1820-1849)

Index of Poets

Barnes, William, *106*
Beddoes, Thomas Lovell, *107, 108*
Blake, William, *28, 30, 60*
Bowles, William Lisle, *36, 38*
Brontë, Emily, *122*
Bryant, W. C., *95*
Burns, George, *32, 33, 34*
Byron, Lord, *72, 77, 82*
Campbell, Thomas, *56*
Carlyle, Thomas, *81*
Chatterton, Thomas, *22*
Clare, John, *89, 90, 91*
Coleridge, Hartley, *102*
Coleridge, Samuel Taylor, *63, 70*
Cowper, William, *19, 21*
Crabbe, George, *23, 24, 25*
Cunningham, John, *17*
Darley, George, *85*
Darwin, Erasmus, *16*
Dyer, George, *11*
Gilpin, William, *15*
Gray, Thomas, *12, 13*
Hemans, Felicia Dorothea, *94*

Hood, Thomas, *103*
Hunt, Leigh, *55, 65*
Keats, John, *96, 97, 100, 101*
Keble, John, *88*
Lamb, Charles, *53*
Landor, Walter Savage, *52*
Mason, William, *14*
Mitford, Mary Russell, *69*
Moore, Thomas, *54*
Palmer, Samuel, *110*
Peacock, Thomas Love, *68*
Poe, Edgar Allan, *112*
Rossetti, Christina, *118*
Salmon, Thomas Stokes, *78*
Schiller, Friedrich von, *81*
Scott, Sir Walter, *48, 49*
Shelley, Percy Bysshe, *83, 84, 87*
Southey, Robert, *50*
Thoreau, Henry David, *116*
Turner, Charles Tennyson, *111*
White, Henry Kirke, *66*
Wilson, John, *52*
Wordsworth, *39, 46, 47*

Index of Artists

Barnett, J., *38*
Barret, George Jnr., *27*
Blake, William, *61*
Buckler, J.C., *38*
Burney, Edward, *53*
Constable, John, *24, 64, 79, 89*
Cotman, J. S., *front endpaper*
Cox, David, *77, 90*
Cozens, J. R., *104-105*
Crome, John, *18, 42*
Danby, Francis, *94, 114-115*
Doughty, Thomas, *117*
Fuseli, Henry, *16, 86*

Girtin, Thomas, *37*
Hunt, W. H., *120-121*
Loutherbourg, P. J. de, *back endpaper*
Martin, John, *56-57*
Palmer, Samuel, *67*
Repton, Humphry, *124*
Russell, John, *85*
Towne, Francis, *62*
Turner, J. M. W., *80*
Varley, John, *82*
Walker, W. and J., *53*
Ward, James, *15*
Wright, Joseph, *frontispece, 73*

'Natural Scenery'. *Humphry Repton*